BARBARA

ITCHING TO CLIMB

Praise for *Itching to Climb*

"Barbara's story is compelling and encouraging and to have accomplished so much, in spite of her eczema is inspiring - particularly to people like me who have first hand experience of it. I've never let eczema stand in my way or stop me from living the way I want and I take my hat off to Barbara and all she has achieved."

Ricky Tomlinson

"Airline pilots view mountains best at a safe distance, thank you, even while we daily climb to the height of Everest in half an hour. Of course we know that physically climbing an actual mountain, up close and personal to the bare rock itself, is much harder and can be very dangerous. You need physical agility and guts, and to do it safely requires much skill and knowledge and team-work.

Meanwhile, we have probably all had an itch that needed scratching at some time in our lives. Luckily, we can hardly conceive of the constant desperate itching that one in 6 of us are born with and have to live with. Welcome to Eczema, which can make you allergic to your own sweat, and cause your skin to be painfully afire, cracked and flaking, weeping or bleeding, simply itching to be scratched. Don't expect much sympathy or understanding from the other 5 in 6 of us who don't have it.

Handicapped by severe eczema, concentrating on rock-climbing is so much more difficult. So how did a woman sufferer of this disabling condition succeed, scoring notable "firsts" in the almost-exclusively-male sport of rock-climbing, in the pre-feminist years following World War 2? How did she later become the first woman to teach in the British Army Junior Leaders School? How did she become the first female to go alone through the Falkland Islands after the war there? How did she become one of the few female pilot's licence holders at the age of 50?

It all took determination, but then Barbara James is a very brave and determined lady. You just have to be focussed, in order to concentrate, when your skin is burning. *Itching to Climb* is her story. You may be humbled by it, as I was."

Robert Dilworth
Airline Captain whose Airbus flight deck
was once visited by the author.

"*Itching to Climb* is a book which should give encouragement to all sufferers of eczema. The author has had to deal with the condition since childhood but has managed to live a full and active life despite the disability. Her desire is that every GP surgery should have a nurse with special training in the treatment of eczema."

Dorothy Lloyd Lewis

"I always knew you had a problem, but you so mastered it that it never intruded, and indeed I never really realised it was serious. I did not know that eczema still had no cure and presumed it was something irritating indeed, but eventually disappeared.

I had been thinking about how at my school everyone mercilessly teased a poor boy who suffered from eczema and was forever scratching. Shows how nasty little boys are, or rather how they do not tolerate anyone they consider abnormal. So I congratulate you on making it the central theme of your book."

John C. Wilkinson, MA, D.Phil, D. Litt, former Reader Oxford University, Emeritus Fellow St Hugh's College.

"For anyone with experience of eczema Barbara's book is a huge inspiration which offers much needed messages of hope. For those without eczema, the book is an absolute must-read as Barbara dispels many of the myths surrounding the condition in an engaging and informative way. She has climbed so many mountains both metaphorically and literally and all the while living with the most severe and often debilitating eczema. Barbara has thrived and succeeded in living many of her wildest dreams, against all the odds. The book is about inspiring and encouraging anyone – not simply those with eczema - and allowing themselves to let their dreams become their realities."

Margaret Cox, Chief Executive, National Eczema Society

"An exciting read by a courageous woman who has achieved so much despite severe eczema."

Dr Robert Jones BDS

"I remember her having bandages on her arms for much of her pre-school years."

Dorothy Barker, aged 93, a lifelong family friend

ENDORSEMENT FOR BARBARA JAMES' BOOK *ITCHING TO CLIMB*

The lives of a substantial proportion of our population, children and adults, are blighted by eczema and allergies. Many fail to reach their potential because of these conditions.

It is then refreshing to read of one sufferer's account of a life full of a wide variety of challenges and achievements often in spite of the absence of appropriate health advice and treatment together with society's failure to understand the conditions.

Barbara James is such a person.

The key moment for her was being introduced to the Snowdonia hills in her teens. Thereafter as climber, instructor and mountain rescue first aider, her employed life was full of challenge.

An early retirement to care for a parent was followed by obtaining a Private Pilot's Licence and further adventures including taking up playing the guitar whilst living in Spain.

Her account, interesting in its own right, will be even more so for those who lack the confidence to break through barriers imposed by health.

Betty Williams

Mrs Betty Williams MP

CYMERADWYAETH I LYFR BARBARA JAMES
ITCHING TO CLIMB

Mae bywydau cyfran helaeth o'n poblogaeth, plant ac oedolion yn cael eu niweidio gan ecsema ac alergeddau. Mae llawer yn methu cyrraedd eu potensial oherwydd y cyflyrau yma.

Felly, mae'n hyfrydwch darllen am adroddiad un dioddefwraig o fywyd llawn amrywiaeth o lwyddiannau a sialensau, yn aml er gwaethaf absenoldeb cyngor a thriniaeth iechyd addas ynghyd a methiant cymdeithas i ddeall y cyflyrau.

Person felly yw Barbara James.

Y foment bwysig iddi oedd cael ei chyflwyno i fryniau Eryri yn ei harddegau. Wedi hynny, fel dringwraig, hyfforddwraig a chymorthydd cymorth cyntaf hefo gwasanaeth achub y mynyddoedd, bu ei bywyd cyflogedig yn llawn sialens.

Yn dilyn ymddeoliad cynnar i ofalu am riant, derbyniodd Drwydded Peilot Preifat's gydag anturiaethau pellach oedd yn cynnwys dysgu chwarae'r gitâr tra'n byw yn Sbaen.

Bydd ei hadroddiad yn ddiddorol i lawer ond hyd yn oed yn fwy diddorol i'r rhai hynny sydd heb yr hyder i dorri trwy'r rhwystrau a trethir gan iechyd.

Betty Williams

Mrs Betty Williams AS

COMMENT ON *ITCHING TO CLIMB*

Though I had been a colleague of Barbara's for some years at St. Mary's College of Education, Bangor, and, later, both her friend and her priest, I had absolutely no idea at all of the richly varied, exciting, dangerous and fascinating life she had lived. Hers is a unique life and experience by any standards. Most men would be totally daunted by the challenges she has faced, the experiences she has lived through and the careers she has pursued. Little wonder, then, that she was a pioneer woman in so many activities normally reserved for the bravest of men.

One would never know this in meeting Barbara James for she is one of the least pushy and most modest and self-effacing of people.

It comes as a double shock to realize that this was all achieved and undertaken, in her typically unfussy and matter-of-fact way, while suffering from the kind of persistent and acute eczema which would have confined many a less gutsy person indoors, or even in bed. Eczema seems to be one of the most common and yet least understood of medical conditions. It is clear from Barbara's experience that knowledge about, and understanding of, this condition needs to be spread more widely, attitudes need changing, and greater and better resources provided. Barbara's unique story is a huge encouragement to all who suffer from a debilitating illness, condition or allergy; but the brutal fact of the lack of resources in schools, in the community and especially in doctor's surgeries and clinics needs to be faced head-on. Why, for example, does my doctor's surgery have an Asthma nurse and Asthma clinics but no specific provision for Eczema which is just as debilitating? This unique story is exciting and nail-biting, funny and sad, infuriating and ultimately triumphant. The Eczema is the grit in the oyster which produces the 'pearl of great price'. Well-written, absorbing and very accessible to people of all temperaments and interests, the book scores on so many levels: adventure, travel, exploration, climbing, adversity and triumph, conflict and resolution, cruelty and kindness. A positive and optimistic book, it is not a only a rattling good read, it is also an inspiration.

Alun J. Hawkins
The Dean of Bangor

SYLWADAU AR Y LLYFR *YSU I DDRINGO*

Er fy mod wedi bod yn gydweithiwr â Barbara am sawl blwyddyn yng Ngholeg Addysg y Santes Fair, Bangor, ac, yn ddiweddarach, yn gyfaill ac yn offeiriad iddi, nid oedd gennyf syniad o gwbl o'r bywyd cyfoethog, amrywiol, cyffrous, peryglus a chyfareddol yr oedd wedi ei gael. Mae ei bywyd a'i phrofiad yn unigryw yn ôl unrhyw safonau. Byddai'r rhan fwyaf o *ddynion* yn dychryn yn llwyr gan yr heriau y mae wedi eu hwynebu, y profiadau y mae wedi byw drwyddynt a thrwy'r gyrfaoedd y mae wedi eu dilyn. Pa ryfeddod, felly, mai hi oedd un o ferched arloesol mewn cymaint o weithgareddau a gedwir yn arferol ar gyfer y dewraf o ddynion.

Ni fyddai neb fyth yn gwybod hynny wrth gyfarfod â Barbara James oherwydd hi yw un o'r rhai lleiaf ymwthiol a mwyaf diymhongar a gwylaidd ymhlith pobl.

Daw'n ddwbl sioc sylweddoli ei bod wedi cyflawni ac ymgymeryd â hyn, yn ei ffordd nodweddiadol ddiffwdan a ddigyffro, tra'i bod yn dioddêf o'r math o ecsema parhaus a llym a fyddai wedi cyfyngu llawer o bobl llai dewr i'r ty, neu hyd yn oed i'r gwely. Mae'n ymddangos bod ecsema'n un o'r cyflyrau meddygol mwyaf cyffredin ac eto sy'n cael ei ddeall leiaf o gyflyrau meddygol. Mae'n eglur o brofiad Barbara bod angen lledaenu'n enhangach y wybodaeth am y cyflwr hwn a dealltwriaeth ohono. Mae angen newid agweddau a darparu mwy a gwell adnoddau. Mae hanes unigryw Barbara yn anogaeth anferth i bawb sy'n dioddef o waeledd, cyflwr neu alergedd gwanychol; ond mae angen wynebu'n uniongyrchol y ffaith giaidd o ddiffyg adnoddau mewn ysgolion, yn y gymuned, ac yn arbennig mewn meddygfeydd a chlinigau meddygon. Pam, er enghraifft, y mae gan feddygfa fy meddyg i nyrs asthma a chlinigau asthma ond dim darpariaeth benodol ar gyfer ecsema sydd yr un mor wanychol? Yn yr hanes unigryw hwn, sy'n gyffroes a chynhyrfus, digrif a thrist, cynddeiriogol a buddugoliaethus yn ei dro, yr ecsema yw'r graean yn y wystysen sy'n cynhyrchu'r 'perl uchel ei bris'. Mae'r llyfr, sydd wedi ei ysgrifennu'n dda, sy'n ddiddorol ac yn hygyrch iawn i bobl o bob anian a diddordeb, yn sgorio ar gymaint o lefelau: antur, teithio, archwilio, dringo, adfyd a buddugoliaeth, gwrthdaro a phenderfyniad, creulondeb a charedigrwydd. Llyfr cadarnhaol ac optimistaidd, sydd nid yn unig yn ddarlleniad da gynddeiriog, ond mae'n ysbrydoliaeth hefyd.

Alun J. Hawkins
Deon Bangor
9th Gorffennaf, 2008

Matador
9 De Montfort Mews
Leicester LE1 7FW, UK
Tel: (+44) 116 255 9311 / 9312
Email: books@troubador.co.uk
Web: www.troubador.co.uk/matador

ISBN 978 1848760 202

A Cataloguing-in-Publication (CIP) catalogue record for this book is available from the British Library.

Front cover photograph. The author in the Dolomites

Typeset in 11pt Bembo by Troubador Publishing Ltd, Leicester, UK
Printed in the UK by TJ International Ltd, Padstow, Cornwall

Matador is an imprint of Troubador Publishing Ltd

To all eczema, allergy and asthma sufferers, their families and friends and to the dermatology specialists, the nurses and the Eczema Society who do their best to help them.

Contents

Acknowledgements

Several years ago I became one those who set off to climb a mountain without adequate preparation and planning. Inevitably the ascent took longer than expected and I needed the help of many guides before finally I reached the summit. Thanks to the Critical Report service provided by the Academi - available only to writers living in Wales and writers in the Welsh language - I decided upon my route.

With Valerie Siviter's invaluable expertise in page layout and Ron and Ginny James' computer skills I could prepare for my first ascent. Gareth Jones and Liz McSweeny read and questioned my navigation errors and the staff in Bangor City's small library helped me when I got lost. Hugh Davis held my rope on some legal bits, Peter Thomas pulled me over financial overhangs and Susan Thompson and Gareth Jones checked my last few steps to the summit; this first ascent was named *Itching to Climb* by Airbus captain Robert Dilworth. Elaine Shea looked after my base camp, Dave Sneath kept it in a good state of repair and Hazel Sneath treated my injuries. Sir Chris Bonnington has been most supportive and Jeremy Thompson and the staff at Troubador Publishing Ltd showed great patience when they received my 'final' and then 'final final' chapters.

Barbara James

Preface

My hope is that this book will interest keen walkers who have never rock climbed, those who have travelled by plane but have never flown one, anyone who fears solo travel and all who would like to share my exploits on St Kilda, in the Falkland Islands and in rural Tenerife.

I was too young to remember much about life in Britain during the Second World War, when women did the jobs of men in agriculture, in factories and a few brave ladies joined the Air Transport Auxiliary. To become a member of the ATC the men had to be medically unable to join the RAF, but fit to fly and all the first twelve females – from which eight were selected - had over 500 hours in their logbooks. A total of 164 ladies ferried huge four-engine Lancaster Bombers, Spitfires and other planes without today's navigation aids, but when the war ended the men needed employment and most females were relegated to housework.

When I left school in 1957 the choice of careers was limited and for many of us, expectations were low. About 2% of the girls in my school went to university and many became a nurse, a teacher or a comptometer operator. (I believe they helped with book keeping by using a machine that was similar to typewriters or a computer key board.) Only with the arrival of the Equal Pay Act (1970) and the Sex Discrimination Act (1975) did opportunities for women in work and in recreation begin to open.

To earn a living as a mountaineer is not easy. Some time after its inauguration the requirements needed to become a British Guide were altered so that they could join the prestigious Union Internationale des Associations des Guides de Montagne. Brede Arkless, born in 1939, was the first British woman to become a guide under the new requirements. Today out of over 170 guides four are female, more women work full time in outdoor pursuit centres and many are becoming famous thanks to their climbing skills. Sadly Brede died of cancer aged only sixty six; her many friends and her eight children miss her wonderful, unique personality.

Today both sexes participate in the most exciting and challenging work places and in recreation. Learning to fly a plane is an expensive hobby so it is no surprise that when I got my Private Pilot's Licence, in 1989, 1,349 males qualified and 78 females; at fifty, I was the oldest of the 17 who were over forty. By 2007, 1,683 men qualified while the number of females has risen to 123, an impressive almost 60% and of these 30 were forty or over.

Without fail, whether walking alone or with friends it is the variety of walks available in the impressive Snowdonia's hills and on the magical Llanddwyn beach that have given me not only great pleasure but also when unhappy their beauty has been therapeutic and comforting. The splendour of the North Wales countryside, the honesty of the weather, usually it rains or the sun shines – long spells of dull, grey days have been few – is addictive. My home has been in Gwynedd for over forty years.

My favourite books

Because they gather dust I keep only a few books. These are very special.

A ladies Life in the Rocky Mountains by Isabella Bird first published in 1880.

True Tales of a Mountain Adventure by Mrs Aubrey Le Bond. First President of the Ladies Alpine Club, 1907-12.

When the Chute went up by Dolly Shepherd, the adventures of an Edwardian parachutist.

The Life and Death of St Kilda by Tom Steel.

Tenerife and its six Satellites by Olivia M. Stone first published in 1889.

Lions, Donkeys and Dinosaurs by Lewis Page.

Foreword

Imagine that mountaineering is your sport and you love animals. But you are allergic to your own sweat, to dogs, cats, pollen and much more.

This book is about overcoming irritated skin and lungs to instruct full time in a mountain school in the 1960s and to train infantry soldiers in the 1970s - when female staff were a rarity. Add to this Barbara explored, solo, islands as different as Tenerife, St Kilda and the Falkland Islands five years after the conflict. When she was told that anyone can learn to fly a plane she did and with her Private Pilot's Licence she enjoyed flying solo around Florida. She has shown considerable courage, immense determination and enthusiasm leavened by a great sense of humour. She is one of the great characters of our rich and diverse climbing family. I hope that her book not only will be an interesting read but also that it will encourage all eczema and allergy sufferers to pursue their goals. I hope that she succeeds.

Chris Bonington

Illustrations

Chapter I
A slow starter

It was no wonder that I found it hard to concentrate on school work. My parents loved fresh air and exercise and they spent all their free time out of doors. By 1953 my father was Captain of Bromborough Golf Club; he longed for me to play but I was fifteen and already my stubborn streak was showing.

The golf club ambience had little to offer a teenager; ladies were banned from the clubhouse bar, while their changing room was a cubby hole well hidden at the back of the building. Mixed foursomes were a rarity and to play and to have tea with ladies had zero appeal. My companions seemed to be small of stature, long in tooth and their chests seemed large enough to defy gravity and the arc of the golf club. Junior members were an unprotected, endangered species. But my parents' sadness when I refused to play golf was nothing compared to their concern when the mountains of Snowdonia became my sports playground.

Today I can understand their worries. I was an only child and poor health had necessitated a very sheltered upbringing. My home on the Wirral was on the outskirts of Willaston, a delightful village with a large green. In its centre was a magnificent copper beech tree that was planted in 1935 to commemorate the Jubilee of King George V; nearby were black and white half-timbered buildings and warm-coloured sandstone walls. Willaston had a thriving church and post office and, even as the village expanded, it retained a relaxed atmosphere of serenity, gentility even. But on Boxing Day the green became a swirling hub of activity when the beagle pack met. Yearly I spent hours working off Christmas dinners by running behind, but out of sight of the hounds and their rare kill.

Many people had businesses in Liverpool; baronial halls were scarce but, like my home, many houses were surrounded by gardens big enough for children to work off their energy without unduly affecting their neighbours. Unlike most families in our road my parents employed no gardener, so our near-acre of land fully occupied their recreation time. Our pond, an old gravel pit, provided fun skating parties for us and our neighbours in winter. Our house was also conveniently near, a five minute drive, for my father to come home for lunch.

The memory of my mother's frequent cry, "Not another meal", still evokes my heartfelt sympathy.

No wonder I never became a dedicated cook!

After the war years I vividly remember being laughed at when I tried to eat the skin of my first banana; I'd never seen one before and we ate the skin of apples! Butter on toast and car travel were luxuries. Many items were in short supply, so everything possible was reused; my mother had a drawer full of brown paper bags and string. My father worked hard to produce our own fruit and vegetables and my parents' influence affects me still. With the help of a wooden mushroom I darn my 100% cotton socks and I prefer vegetables to flowers in my garden - but I've drawn the line at keeping two turkeys in the garage for Christmas, as my father did in those years of food shortages!

My paternal grandmother, Grandma Lunt, died in the 1918 flu epidemic and both my father and his only sister, Elsie, had the Lunt family's lovely brown eyes and good looks. Elsie lived with and cared for Grandpa Lunt in a small, end-of-terrace house near the pumping station at Hooton where, like his father before him, my father was superintendent.

When I hear the faint cries for water meters today I remember that throughout my childhood my father's frequently repeated words were, "Water is the cheapest commodity that we have and it should be metered like electricity."

Mother was the third of seven children, the eldest being her brother, Arthur, who had six sisters. Her father, Grandpa Speight, became Technical Director of Spillers Milling, one of the famous British flour milling groups. With an office in the splendid Cunard Building in Liverpool and a good salary, he was one of the lucky few who, pre-war, could drive his family from the Wirral to walk up Snowdon or to visit other interesting, lovely places. He died before retiring, aged 68, and when I look in the mirror I picture Grandma Speight playing bridge with a cigarette permanently in her mouth and a glass of whisky to hand. I inherited the Speight family's long face that in later years crinkled between the wrinkles, their addiction to dark chocolate, but luckily not a love of whisky or cigarettes.

However it would have been a miracle if I'd not inherited allergies and eczema. My father was allergic to artificial materials and to horses;

My parents, Tom and Eileen Lunt, in 1962.
They were en route to the wedding of Jane Barker, daughter of their good friends Bill and Dorothy.

he sneezed when he was near them, or even when he was near to the horse riders wearing their riding clothes! Although my mother did not suffer from either, there was eczema and psoriasis in her family. I remember little of my childhood years other than standing on the bathroom stool while my mother used nappy pins to imprison my arms in an improvised strait jacket, made from a pillow case; this stopped me from scratching in my sleep. I was five or six when I was hospitalised with a severe streptococcal infection - and if my memory is correct it was penicillin that saved my life. Mother's worries about me were great and, like all mothers, she looked everywhere for help. I have no idea how much money she spent taking me at regular intervals to the latest herbalist who claimed to have a cure. But I do know that, due to people's lack of understanding, she was frequently told, "You're being a fussy mother because you have only one child."

Because our doctor had promised that I'd grow out of my eczema, my mother also had to endure my frequently repeated question, "When will I get better?"

I was lucky. As I got older the severity of my eczema did lessen, but it never went away. Before I started school at the age of seven the strait jacket was no longer needed. Instead the sleeves of my pure cotton pyjamas had mitts and luckily they too were unnecessary by my teens. It was not until I started school that I became aware that I was the one thing all children hate, I was different. I was very unhappy because I couldn't go to parties where there was a dog or cat in the house and when I could go, I had to tell people that I couldn't eat certain foods.

When I asked my mother about my problems she said, "When you were a baby and your arms were outside the pram covers, raindrops falling on your skin caused itchy lumps."

Even today sweat causes the same reaction as raindrops, unstoppable itching. In June, when the pollen season coincided with important exams, I had difficulty breathing and itchy eyes. I suspect that some of my mother's worries were soothed by a doctor neighbour.

Ruth Dovey said, "Having eczema will make her strong."

It has.

Although my health had improved by my early teens, at school I was interested only in sports until a new, young, inspiring biology teacher, Miss Taylor, arrived. Her lively personality and tremendous enthusiasm for her subject transformed a failing student, with low self esteem, into a hard working one. I will never cease to be grateful because, thanks to her, I surprised my teachers and my parents by gaining five 'O' levels. Now my frustrations arose more from living far from my class mates rather than from my eczema. I was unable to join in their normal adolescent activities, whether it was going to the cinema or a dance, without the ignominy of being collected by a parent.

When I was ten Grandpa Lunt had promised me a pony if I grew out of my allergy so, despite my mother's warnings, I'd insisted on riding. I needed to experience, many times, all the wheezing and itching associated with being on a horse before I was convinced that it was impossible for me to have the pony that I'd longed for. Luckily as I entered the sixth form, this stubborn determination was put to good use and I took full advantage of Birkenhead High School's excellent academic opportunities. I worked harder than I'd ever worked before. Founded in 1885, the school is now part of the UK's largest independent schools' network, the Girls' Day School Trust (GDST).

I was in my second year in the sixth form, still uncertain where to go in life, when my wheel of fortune jumped a sprocket. There might have been discussions with my parents going on behind my back, but if they were I knew nothing. I was totally taken by surprise when my PE teacher, Mrs Elsby, decided to take me, alone, for my half term in February 1957 to a mountaineering centre in Capel Curig. It was to change my life for ever.

Chapter 2
Life Changes in Capel Curig

For many years, when en route to our annual family two-week holiday in a caravan beside a superb beach near Abersoch, we ate our picnic lunch beside Llynnau Mymbyr, the lake near Capel Curig. In those days it was considered a long drive so, with a map from the AA, my father planned where to have our midway rest stop. Here, with luck and a clear day, we enjoyed the splendid view of Snowdon, at 3560ft (1085m) the highest peak in Wales, and the adjacent summits that formed the famous Snowdon horseshoe. But I had no ambition to climb them. Hill walking was not an activity done by our family or friends so I doubt very much if, without Mrs Elsby's initiative, I would have discovered mountains.

Plas y Brenin, the National Mountaineering Centre (formally the Central Council of Physical Recreation Centre) held courses in a variety of activities including rock climbing, canoeing and horse riding. But on that Saturday in February, very fit military personnel had arrived for a week's general mountaineering course. On my first mountain day I discovered that, despite my daily mile-long walk to and from Hooton station, to catch the train to school, my fitness level was low.

I was ill prepared for this strenuous activity. Struggling up the steep, rocky Bristly Ridge to Glyder Fach, about 2000ft (610m) above the road, I was on the limit of my strength. Looking upwards, I occasionally caught a glimpse of our group. I was a long way behind them, I could do nothing about it, but I was lucky.

A member of the group said, "I'll stay with you and be tail-end Charlie."

This person was appointed, by responsible leaders, to look after anyone finding it difficult to keep up with the stronger walkers.

Our leader was a *voluntary* instructor; he had paid for his board in order to work at the centre. It was obvious that his concentration was focused more on not being overtaken by the fit soldiers and less on looking after the weaker members of his group. As those in the lead battled it out, the distance between us increased and I knew that it was only my helper's constant encouragement that kept me going.

When I thanked him for his kindness, his only comment was, "If I'm not at the front I might as well be at the back."

Because I couldn't see the summit, the steep, rocky ridge seemed to go on for ever but relief came abruptly with flat, stony ground that led to the summit pile of rocks. Here we all perched, like birds on a branch, near the end of a weirdly balanced horizontal 'cantilever' stone. At last I could let my pounding heart return to normal and give my aching muscles time to stop hurting. But I did not have long. The group had arrived long before us and all too soon the leader set off again.

Capel Curig Pinnacles

The rocks where I made my first tentative attempts to climb.

On this course I discovered that muscle weakness was not my only problem. At seventeen my social skills were underdeveloped. My innocence must have shone like a beacon and I found it difficult to socialise in the bar with soldiers who had travelled far and seen much. The day's activities had tired me, so, after the lecture that followed the evening meal, I took the easy option. I went to bed early.

However, while sharing experiences on the hill I was surprised and pleased that with some instructors, a companionable atmosphere developed within the group. When I had enough breath to talk, I found it much easier to have, and even to initiate, conversations with strangers. My shyness and reserve disappeared as if by magic, albeit temporarily, and this outweighed the physical hardships. I revelled in every hill day being a new experience. The mountains showed off their extensive wardrobe, changing from pleasant conditions to cold and windy. When it rained all the summits hid beneath a thick blanket of threatening cloud. Then a heavy snowfall transformed everything.

In dazzling sunshine I made my first, floundering attempts to ski on the gentle slopes of the Carneddau Mountains, which looked down on the Ogwen Valley. The skis persisted in depositing us not only on the soft snow but also on uncovered, bruising rocks, so I was thankful that we had plenty of rest breaks. While my lungs relished the clean air, I admired the crystal clear summits of Tryfan and the Glyders in razor sharp outline across the valley. I listened, fascinated, to our wonderful instructor, Tim Aaron, a salaried, permanent member of staff. He described his special feelings for mountains in general and for the Carneddau in particular. It was obvious that he wanted everyone in his group to enjoy the day and for his professionalism I am eternally grateful. I caught his infectious love of the Snowdonia hills. Yet it was an experience that I so nearly missed.

When our half term ended on Wednesday, midway through the course, Mrs Elsby returned alone to the Wirral. Her courageous action surprised me because to be absent from school at any time required parental notes in triplicate. Also this disciplinarian was a stickler for etiquette. Bad manners would put even the best player out of the tennis team. Yet Mrs Elsby left me in Wales to finish the course, a major reversal of her code of behaviour. She faced our headmistress, my father, who was sure that I would be expelled, and my mother - who never ceased to blame her for introducing me to mountains! But her instincts were good. She could see that I was ready to 'fly the nest'.

Before the course had ended, I was wondering how I could return to Capel Curig when I noticed some outbuildings across the road from Plas y Brenin. On a door, writ large, were the words 'Chester Mountaineering Club'. This gave me hope because my home was within easy reach of Chester. I couldn't find the club's number in the telephone directory, but I was determined not to lose this possible route back to the hills. I wrote a letter right away, drew a map of Capel Curig on the envelope, marked the spot with a cross and, after some agonising weeks, I was relieved to have a reply.

The letter had reached the secretary and with a school friend, Adrienne Roberts, I chatted with CMC members in a pub in Chester. That night Adrienne met her husband-to-be, Keith, and I found the route to a lifetime pursuing – or being dropped into – work and play that was mainly the prerogative of men. At that moment, neither of us realised the impact that meeting would have on our lives; my 'A' level exams were a few months away and the mountains had to wait.

I had difficulty choosing a career. Physiotherapy appealed to me but the pay was low. I had no burning desire to teach, however, the long school holidays were too good to miss and the decision was made. Then my mother insisted that I applied to Homerton, a teacher training college in Cambridge - where she hoped that I would meet suitable young men! By the time my rejection letter arrived I had the choice of waiting a year and reapplying, or going to whatever college still had places available. When I passed 'A' level Zoology and English, I decided not to wait another year.

In September 1957, I went to C.F. Mott Teacher Training College on the outskirts of Liverpool. All through my childhood I'd felt different from other children and I was very aware that my unusual name, 'Barbarajane', didn't help. Mother had gone to visit friends in America and their daughter, my namesake, 'Barbarajane', had, by one of those quirks of fate, perfect peaches-and-cream skin. I'd always disliked my name so at college I became 'Barbara'.

Resident in a hostel we endured a prison-like routine with twenty-four hour control. Meals were compulsory and we had to sign in and stay in the hostel from 10.30pm until breakfast time. After the evening meal, at 6.30pm, we dashed out to catch a bus to the nearest cinema, saw the end of the film, sat through the interval and watched the beginning before rushing back to college to be locked in. At the time when you wanted to spread your wings, they were well and truly clipped!

I was disappointed to find that the college course was neither challenging (we repeated the nitrogen cycle that we had done at school) nor of much future use - the floral formula of a primrose was of little relevance to teenagers! However, one fact from the education classes helps me now: whenever possible avoid making difficult requests on Monday mornings. A positive response would be more likely on a Thursday afternoon, when the week was nearly over and the weekend was near, but not too near.

Luckily for me, when Mrs Elsby's daughter, Jane, was a student, she'd worked as a waitress in the Tyn y Coed Hotel; on the opposite side of the road there was an eye-catching stage coach. That Jane had done this work overcame my mother's doubts about her daughter being a waitress in Capel Curig. This attractive village had slate-roofed cottages alongside Thomas Telford's famous (and the little changed) London to Holyhead, A5 road. In its construction, Telford, born in 1757, was challenged first by mountainous terrain and then by the fast flowing, strong currents of the Menai Straits at Bangor. Here, this brilliant engineer replaced a ferry with a majestic suspension bridge that, to the relief of all travellers, was completed in 1826. In 1785, fifty-five people on the ferry had been stranded on a sand bar and all but one was dead by the time rescuers reached them next day.

I started work on a very busy Easter Friday and I soon discovered the quirky humour that flourished among hotel staff. When things got very busy *my* prepared coffee tray might disappear for *their* clients while my back was turned. But their good company more than compensated for their tricks and my low pay – the owner, Mrs Newman, expected customers to give us good tips!

After work on Thursday evenings I listened in the bar, awed by the superb Welsh singing, led by the good looking family from Rhos Farm, brothers Alan and Gwilym Jones and their sister, Lynn. I was car-less so, whenever possible, Lynn and I organised our days off to coincide. Hitch hiking was not uncommon and Shell tankers from the Wirral passed the hotel front door en route to RAF Valley. Here the kind drivers dropped us off at the beach nearby, we sunbathed, had a picnic and later we were collected and delivered safely back to the hotel.

Hotel work had enabled me to return to Capel Curig during college holidays. But only when I discovered that the last Girls' Outward Bound Course was to be held at Plas y Brenin, from 20th October to 15th November 1958, could I return there in term time. Already there were centres for boys and one for Girls' Outward Bound was soon to open. It was perfect timing for my education thesis. I had to pay for my accommodation and my college paid for my travel for two visits, a weekend and for half term week. How to get there was not solved as easily because in the 1950s public transport was the norm, bicycles were used mostly to get to work and car ownership was still a luxury.

Luckily, for my weekend visit to Plas y Brenin, a bus ran from Chester to Capel Curig via a circuitous route through Wrexham and Llangollen. But this service did not run midweek. For my half term visit, my education thesis recorded my amazing lack of planning:

"On Thursday 30th October I had bad luck travelling and it took me 7 hours to get there. It had its compensations however, for I had a lovely walk. I managed to get a bus from Bangor station to Bethesda. This left me about 10 more miles. I had a lift to Lake Ogwen, 5 miles, and then I started walking with Tryfan towering above me on the right and Lake Ogwen shining in the moonlight on the left. The moon was very bright but was covered intermittently by passing clouds. I did not meet anyone and thoroughly enjoyed the walk. However, it was getting late so when I saw a phone box I phoned for a taxi – and I was driven the last few miles in state." I was worried about missing the meal and oblivious of any possible dangers.

The aim of the Outward Bound movement is 'to inspire individuals to fulfil their potential through challenging experiences'. In keeping with the era, guitar-accompanied folk singing social evenings ended at 10pm. Sundays were rest days when we went to church and then the students ensured that their personal log books were up to date; they'd be seen by their sponsors. The Outward Bound Principal, Miss Martin, arranged centre transport first to early communion services, at the

Catholic and Anglican churches in Betws y Coed, about 5 miles away, and then to the 10am Welsh and 11am English services in Capel Curig.

During the remainder of the day, I took the opportunity to chat to the girls. June Gazzard from Bristol told me that on her journey to the course she was so scared that she spoke to no one and was near to tears. But meeting others in the same position had consoled her. Now I could hardly 'get a word in edgeways' before we were called indoors to practise hymn singing for a service in the evening, taken by the Chaplain of St Mary's College in Bangor.

All those on the course were young; some were still at school but most were from a variety of jobs in industry, sales and the Health Service. Whatever their background, they had to do all the activities. Many girls were lively and full of fun, others were quiet and retiring and few had any experience of outdoor activities. I was impressed by how those who were afraid managed to overcome their fear to varying degrees. A small, thin, quiet girl with black hair, Jessie Christie, couldn't swim and was very scared of water. But as we emptied the canoes, the air resounded with shouts and laughter and Jessie's voice was as loud as the others. My only regret was that I did not have time to investigate how much a report, adverse or otherwise, from a four-week course might affect that person's future career.

I doubt if any other student had gained so much from writing their education thesis. I'd increased my confidence to travel alone, my ability to talk to strangers and not least I'd gained my experience in outdoor activities. After years of being restricted by poor health at last I had found what I really wanted to do, to be near to the mountains of Snowdonia.

Student 'life' had been non-existent at C.F. Mott and I felt that I'd been robbed of any fun. Teacher training was about to change from a two to a three year course so I managed to convince my parents that I needed another year in training at Normal College, Bangor! Here there were two teacher training colleges and a university college - students were plentiful! My education thesis had ended: "*I am extremely interested in the Outward Bound movement and I would like to work for them, either as a temporary instructor or as a permanent instructor*". I had taken a small step towards my wish being granted.

Chapter 3

Losses and gains in North Wales

A kind old Welsh lady lived in a tiny terraced house in Park Street, just below College Road, Bangor. Here twin beds had been squeezed into the small attic bedroom that I shared with another student, Hilary Peters, from Haverford West. Hilary, attractive and dark haired, was about my age and her plans for the future, unlike mine, were secure. She was to marry Alf after the course had ended.

Our five minute walk to Bangor Normal College's dining hall was no hardship, even in the winter months. Many years earlier a prospective student had received a letter from the college saying, 'Bangor is a wet and windy place, come prepared'. I had. But being accustomed to peaceful breakfasts, the penetrating voices of girls from the Caernarfon area had to be avoided. As tactfully as possible I manoeuvred to sit next to students from the south Wales with attractive gentle accents.

I remember little about the course other than having to endure yet another interminably long lecture on the nitrogen cycle. But an unspoilt beach with unrivalled views near Newborough has given me, and my mother, comfort in times of grief ever since. Not far from the village centre a mile-long sandy track through trees led to the beach; later this path was replaced by a tarmac road, complete with sleeping policemen. Emerging from the wood to left and right, making the walk worthwhile, there were miles of magnificent golden sand and a promontory, Llanddwyn Island. This was part of Newborough Warren Nature Reserve that became detached from the mainland when tides were at their highest.

St Dwynwen is the Welsh patron saint of lovers, whose feast day is celebrated on the 25th January. On the 'island' there was a chapel, now ruined, that was built on the site of Dwynwen's original chapel. And at the end of the promontory there was a life boat station, built in 1840, and a lighthouse that had replaced a beacon in 1845. The nearby cannon summoned the crew who saved 101 lives before the lifeboat station was closed in 1903. The cannon and a lighthouse remain. As if this 'island' and coastline wasn't perfection, there were panoramic views of the Snowdonia Mountains. The beach was a hidden gem; I loved it, but the infrequent bus times and the long walk made it a major outing.

It was during Rag Week, when students went mad and did outrageous things to raise money for charity, that I had my first, and last, experience of playing in a women's rugby team. Most of us didn't know anything about the game and we all found having instructions for our every move shouted at us from the sideline a hilarious experience. But because all the girls had boy friends I still felt an odd man out, until one was found for me - by another student! To protect his identity I will call him Arthur.

Arthur was a solidly built, jovial local character with that all important thing, transport. After his briefing, about which way to lean on bends when travelling at speed on his motor bike, I hugged his ample waist. He felt like a cuddly teddy bear. I was happy to have a companion at last but despite his many kisses and gropings, our relationship remained innocent until the course was nearly over.

It was a lovely June evening when he took me for a well-wined meal at the Gazelle Hotel, situated on the Menai Straits, with a stunning view of the mountains. Afterwards, incapable of resistance, I allowed myself to be led into Siliwen woods, not far from my lodgings, and once back in my room I realised what I had done. I knew nothing about contraception and, for a week, I was a very frightened lady. I was sleep deprived and fear of pregnancy and what it would do to my parents filled my days with horror. However, once I knew that I had 'got away with it', a phrase in use in those days, he never succeeded in luring me into the woods again despite his best efforts. Our relationship ended when I left Bangor but his prophecy, that I would always return to North Wales, came true.

Now a freshly minted schoolmistress, I worried about how I'd cope with teaching biology at Bromborough Secondary Modern School. But as I cycled from home to work I remembered that my transformation from a non-achieving pupil to a hard working one was thanks to one teacher. Miss Taylor's unfailing enthusiasm was impressive. To find a special nerve she'd dug her shapely nails into a dogfish week after week despite the overpowering and unpleasant smell of fish and formalin.

I wanted all my classes to see a real heart surrounded by lungs, not just diagrams of organs, or floral formula, in a biology book! Local butchers generously responded to my frequent requests for eyes and hearts, but laboratory assistants, to prepare and clear up experiments after successive classes, were non-existent. It was impossible for pupils to do practical work individually so I compromised. Whenever possible, they helped me with the dissection that was done on my front bench. This was better than their having no practical at all.

Teacher training courses had concentrated on academic subjects; I remember no advice about class management and if there had been, I doubt that it would have included how to handle living and dead animals. Guinea pigs at the back of my classroom provided much entertainment and information before a baby was born. One day I gave priority to explanation over attention to guinea pig squeaks and, to the laughter of the class, it wet my skirt. The poor thing *had* tried to warn me! All cockroaches were dead cockroaches after live ones escaped from the jar - many managed to disappear up the long sleeves of girls' blouses! Offers of eyes from the abattoir were refused after the pupil who worked there marched into the classroom with two eyes still in the cow's skinned head; removing them wasn't easy.

I found teaching very hard work. To talk for over six hours a day was a strain, I had frequent sore throats and when I caught whooping cough, teaching was impossible. Inevitably my eczema worsened in direct proportion to my level of tiredness, so I was very grateful that my mother presented me with meals on the table and a shopping-free lifestyle. After a hectic day, I had energy left only for the essentials, lesson preparation and marking class work before heading exhausted to bed. I likened teaching with enthusiasm to being on a stage all day. On the rare occasions that I could find transport, I spent weekends in Wales.

It was here that I met Anne (not her real name). This intelligent lady had impressed me not only by regularly driving her Tiger Cub motorbike from London to Snowdonia, but also with her rapier-like assessments of the personalities we met. So when she suggested going to Skye, I jumped at the opportunity to visit somewhere new. We planned to meet at a campsite in Keswick and this we did.

Next morning Anne checked her bike, topped up the petrol and bought a spare can of oil. Soon I knew why. Burdened by the weight of two people, the bike used all the oil on the 44 miles (71km) to Gretna Green on the Scottish border. To lighten the load we decided that I would take the food and hitchhike, she would keep the tent and we would meet in Glasgow.

I didn't have to wait long for a lift and as we approached Glasgow my concerned driver asked, "Where do you want to be dropped off?"

Only then did I realise that no meeting place had been arranged.

His suggestion, "Because all traffic passes through Trongate, it would be the best place for you to wait", seemed sensible.

I had no choice but to accept his advice.

For two hours I stood, alone, while trying to ignore the comments of the drunks pouring out of the pubs at 9pm closing time. But the relief that flooded through me when I saw Anne approaching was fleeting because, concentrating on the traffic, she did not see me. Seconds later she'd disappeared from view.

To go to the police station for help was the only thing that I could think of and here, despite my message being sent by ticker-tape to other police stations, they could find no news of her whereabouts.

The harassed policeman said, "I can't help you any more, go to the Youth Hostel."

I did. But it was full and neither a message from Anne nor a bed awaited me. By now it was late and I was really frightened. I had no idea what to do next when a man approached me.

He asked, "Have you anywhere to go for the night?"

I replied, "No."

I followed him, and the three other girls that he'd collected, to a Salvation Army hostel. This man led us to safe accommodation, a clean bed and a filling breakfast. Recovered from my fright next morning I decided to continue the journey. I caught a bus to the outskirts of Glasgow and from there I started to hitch hike to Skye.

It took me 5 hours to travel a mere 50 miles (80kms) to Tyndrum where I stood, mapless and planless. It was beginning to dawn on me that going to Skye might not be a good idea, when again my luck turned. I was offered a lift with a man and his son who were going to join their family, his wife and two daughters, at Fort William. In return for their kind invitation to sleep that night in their tent I gratefully shared my steak and bacon with them.

Energised by good food, safe sleep and not least by their generosity, I got a lift along the single line road's 40 miles (64kms) to Mallaig. Here I caught the ferry to Armadale pier where I was shocked to have to pay two pence - to walk the few yards of its length to set foot on Skye! A Macbraynes coach was the only transport to Sligachan, an isolated pub that was miles from anywhere and here I stood waiting beside a deserted bus. Eventually the driver, Terry, emerged to take me to Glenbrittle where I hoped that Chester Mountaineering Club member, Roy Rimmer, would still be working with a well known local boatman, Ron MacDonald.

Pony on the Carneddau hills
They descend to the lower slopes in bad weather.

Anne's journey had not been trouble free either. Her head had lost an argument with a pavement, but despite concussion keeping her in a casualty unit overnight, next day this tough lady signed herself out of hospital. When, finally, she had tracked down her bike she discovered that the ignition had been left on and the battery was flat. Undaunted, with the battery charged and the oil leak solved – by pushing a piece of silver paper up the leaking tube - she too arrived at Glenbrittle. Her lonely tent was easy to spot. I was shocked to hear about her troubles, the last of which was Ron's cow putting its foot through the wall of her tiny tent and eating her bread. To give Anne more space I was glad to accept the kind offer of Ron and his wife to sleep on their lounge floor. The added advantage was an escape from Skye's famous midges.

Sadly we never did set foot on the Cuillin ridge because the weather was as wet as Skye can be. But we did have two magical, rain-free days when we saw Skye at its best. While our things dried, we enjoyed the fabulous views of the Cuillin ridge during a boat trip to Rum with Ron and Roy. Rum had supported a thriving community until it was 'cleared', late in the nineteenth century, to make way for sheep and deer. In 1957 the island was bought by the Nature Conservancy Council, now called the Scottish Natural Heritage.

The memorable Skye trip convinced me that I needed some transport. With an annual salary of £534 and giving £3 weekly to my mother for my keep, a well used, decrepit, second hand 90cc scooter was all that I could afford. But it was severely underpowered. From Willaston, my journey to Capel Curig took 4 hours, now about 90 minutes in a car. Climbing the hill from Bethesda to Ogwen in a head wind the scooter ran out of puff and I was forced to 'walk' while still sitting on it.

No journey was trouble free. The clutch cable broke on one trip, the brake cable on the next. Because both were splendidly repaired by the good Hughes Brothers garage in Capel Curig, I accepted these happenings. But the same could not be said for my parents. Their nerves were unable to stand the strain. They bought me a Mini van that had a 40mph maximum speed limit and I repaid them in instalments. However, for my parents it was an own goal. Now that my weekends in the hills were not dictated by the weather, they became more frequent!

Sleeping away from home was never easy. To stay in my van cost nothing – but a night's scratching! To reduce itching I needed clean skin before going to bed, plenty of hot water for a good wash, or preferably a bath. In bed and breakfast accommodation, if a dog had stayed in the room before me, I would have paid for a wheezing, sleepless night. Luckily the Chester Mountaineering Club (CMC) hut cost was minimal, there was a comfy bunk bed in the women's dormitory and the cooking facilities provided plenty of hot water.

I was very aware of my lack of fitness and I had a dread of holding back others on hill walks, while dangling on the end of a rope after a fall on an easy rock climb had frightened me, so usually I went walking alone. Without a map and unaware of the risks, I followed unknown groups into cloud. If climbing magazines or other sources of information and advice were available, I didn't find them and it was only when Jean Cropp, the PE teacher at my school, heard about my exploits and joined me that I had found a companion at last.

Female mountaineers were few and the climbers' bars in Capel Curig were a barren hunting ground for the predatory single males, especially when members of the RAF Valley Mountain Rescue Team were nearby. Led by their good looking, chain-smoking team leader, Tony Bennett, they spent many weekends camping in different places in Snowdonia. It was not long before we were warned that they had a girl in every village! But eventually we accepted their invitation to join them at their campsite for some great singsongs that were well fuelled by their for-emergency-use-only, firewater strong rum! Jean met, and later married, a Team member, talented guitar player Bob England and I met Mick Mills, a kind, bespectacled pipe smoker.

It was in the Tyn y Coed bar that a friend drew my attention to another climber.

She surprised me by leaping up saying, "That's Ron James, I must buy him a drink."

He was slim, of average height and he too wore glasses – but he was not as good looking as Mick! Not long afterwards Jean and I were staying at the CMC hut, bad weather made hill walks impossible and it was too early to go to a pub. So we went to Capel Pinnacles, small rocks a few minutes walk above Capel Curig crossroads. Here beginners were being introduced to rock climbing, by Ron James.

He said, "The October Fair is on this evening in Menai Bridge."

With intent, he suggested that it would be safer to leave my Mini van at Ogwen Cottage, the mountain school where he lived and was Chief Instructor. We were glad to save petrol so we travelled in his centre transport to the fair. Here Ron met his girl friend, Heather, and we met Mick, Bob and the Team. But before we'd left Ogwen Cottage to return to the CMC hut I'd accepted Ron's invitation to climb with him.

From then on, when Ron was not guiding clients, I climbed with him. I discovered the pleasure of moving up steep rock and I was amazed that our first route together was a VS, a very severe climb. With safety in mind his every move was calculated and my fears of rock climbing disappeared; I was thrilled to feel my climbing technique improving and my body getting stronger.

It was at the end of our first year in teaching that Jean and I decided to visit Mutters in Austria. One-month package holidays were not available, so we combined two two-weeks together and this gave us some very welcome extra spending money from the refunded, unused return flight. The time passed pleasantly but, never one for 'resting and relaxing', I looked forward to the arrival of Ron and Tony Bennett, en route to climb in the Italian Dolomites, near Cortina d'Ampezzo. I was surprised and delighted when they offered to squeeze us into their Mini and sad that, after a disagreement with Tony, Jean decided not to go for this three-night visit. She missed an exciting trip.

The track to the Auronzo hut was narrow, rough and steep with a huge drop on one side; the Mini struggled for a grip on the stony surface until Tony kept the wheels on the ground by sitting on the bonnet. Eventually we reached the campsite.

Here Ron said, "Hut dormitories vibrate with orchestra-loud snores and down drafts of garlic waft everywhere."

We squeezed into one tent.

After an uncomfortable night they left early and when, finally, I woke up their voices drew my eyes upwards. Two tiny figures were mere specks on the Tre Cima de Lavarado. I thought they were mad because this spectacular lump of rock rose vertically, 1640ft (500m) above rolling, grassy slopes. Next day I was frightened when we walked on a wide path to look up at the steep great North Face. Its top chimneys overhung the base to such an extent that stones, loosened by unseen climbers high on the wall, fell *outside* the downhill edge of the path. It never occurred to me then that a lot more dangerous was our very drunken drive, in a rainstorm, over the old Brenner Pass with a bottle of Chianti – that was empty before we reached Mutters!

It was after Mick's posting to Singapore ended our innocent friendship that my relationship with Ron became more than a climbing partnership and without a second thought I accepted his invitation to go with him to the Alps. Here he planned to meet and guide Jack Hampson, a charming teacher from Taunton School, who wanted to climb the dramatic peak, Dent du Geant. An exciting cable car ride took us from Courmayeur to a stunning panoramic view of mountains and glaciers and the Torino hut at 10,827ft (3,300m). Immediately I felt different. My lungs always became distressed when the air was full of pollen and pollution, but here I could breathe so deeply that I left Ron behind on the steep walk from the cable car station to the hut. This surprised us both.

The hut's toilet was horrific. It resembled a hanging basket. Securely attached to the edge of the rock, overhanging an enormous drop, was a box with a hole in the floor. Through it, if the wind blew in a certain direction, toilet paper was blown upwards so to hand was a stick to push everything down. From then on, toilets became a feature of our time in rural Italy. Before we had a meal, while Ron ordered a drink, I inspected the toilet. On this depended whether or not we ate there.

Another part of my Alpine apprenticeship was solo route finding. I watched Ron and Arabic-speaking John Wilkinson (he could do a splendid belch while saying hum-de-le-la) climb the steep 2,625ft (800m) Grade V1+ Tofana de Rozes. Once they'd passed the hardest section of the route, I knew they would reach the top. Walking downhill wearing their light, tight-fitting climbing shoes was painful so I found the way to the summit to meet them, carrying their comfy walking boots. Later Ron repeated this climb with me.

I'd been regularly scanning the *Times Educational Supplement* when, in spring 1964, Wolverhampton Education Authority advertised for instructors. I was thrilled to be selected for an interview at the Towers Outdoor Pursuit Centre, hidden in the woods between Capel Curig and Betws y Coed. On the day that Harold Drasdo was appointed Warden, Ken Rudram, a skilled canoeist, and I accepted the posts of Assistant Wardens.

By the time my summer term ended, I'd had four years at Bromborough School; Ron was already in Chamonix. So I flew to Geneva airport, found a hotel for the night, a bus to Chamonix, the campsite and finally, our tent. Inside I was shocked to see his favourite yellow T-shirt, stained with blood. But he wasn't there. The wait seemed an eternity before I saw him returning and relief flooded through me. He'd been hit on a shoulder by a falling stone; he had difficulty moving that arm, but it could have been much worse. And the bonus was that when he was fit enough we did my first long, high Alpine route, the Midi-Plan traverse at about 12,000ft (3650m).

At the Midi cable car top station's exit tunnel, the early morning cold made my fingers fumble as I tightened the straps of my crampons. These downward pointing spikes beneath my boots would dig into the ice slope as I inched my way down the first steep, unavoidable, treacherous and very exposed slope – for me the most frightening part of the whole route. Only when we reached the col, a saddle between two hills with a drop on each side, was I allowed a moment's pause. The sun was warm and mountain scenery was stunning while 9,000ft (2740m) below, the Chamonix valley was still in darkness. From then on as we progressed along the ridge the temperature varied enormously between freezing cold (the shady side) and scorching, scratching-hot (the sunny side).

We were descending from the Plan, roped together, glissading, a standing slide down the snow, when Ron caught my heels and we both fell. The sun-softened slope had caused snowballs to form under his crampons making them gripless. Roped together we slid downhill, alternately stopping each other's fall with our ice axes for a second before the weight of the other jerked the axe out of the snow. I had a worm's eye view of a crevasse, a dangerous crack in a glacier, before we stopped, shaken but not hurt, and took off our now useless crampons.

From then on there was never a minute to stop and admire the famous mountain views. Our descent of the Valley Blanche glacier became an eternity of watching every step to avoid falling into bottomless, dangerous crevasses. I knew that if I stopped, I wouldn't be able to start again and back at base I did seize up; but the great experience was worth every ache. I looked forward to my new job in Capel Curig.

Chapter 4
Living in, working outside

I was thrilled when, in September 1964, my years of commuting to North Wales ended. I'd exchanged the classroom's lung-irritating chalk dust for a magnificent outdoor classroom, the Snowdonia Mountains.

Until I got fit I expected to find the work physically tiring but the Towers' daily routine was more relaxed than I expected, our students chose what they did every day. When all the places for canoeing, thought the easiest option, were taken their choice wavered between rock climbing, believed to be dangerous, and hill walking, known to be hard work. I switched the contents of my rucksack in rhythm with their changes of mind until the final decision was made!

Some weeks I summitted many of the 14 peaks over 3,000ft (914m) with very fit, all-male groups. At first their preferred walking speed exceeded mine, but I knew that I was getting stronger when low level walks, through the woods around Betws y Coed, became work rather than a pleasant respite from the high hills. Rock climbing definitely increased the muscles in my arms. I had three students and on every pitch, a section of the climb, I pulled up three 120ft ropes; we did between six and eight pitches so by end of the day, depending on the climb, I hauled up 2,000-3,000ft of rope. Luckily I never had another instructor's experience, a strong bell-ringer pull on his rope while climbing;

He shouted down to his pupil, "What's the matter?"

"I want to go to the toilet", was the girl's reply.

With a pleasant breeze and sunny but not hot weather, outdoor work was a pleasure that was enhanced when we had the hills to ourselves in term times. If the group appreciated the stunning scenery then the day was very rewarding. However, Capel Curig was famous for its high rainfall records. When a spell of continuous wet days coincided with a high percentage of students coming on the course only because their friends were coming, then it was hard work.

Their oft repeated cry was, "How much farther is it?"

I was enjoying both my work and my partnership with Ron when that winter, unexpectedly, his behaviour changed. I thought our relationship was over so, needing to get away, at Christmas I went alone to Aviemore for a week's skiing. Snow conditions were good and the evenings were pleasantly filled chatting with a handsome, if overweight, Scottish television presenter until one evening when I was called to the phone. It was Ron asking me to marry him. My heart leapt. I said, "Yes, I'll be back at the end of the week!"

My tiny bedroom in the Towers was near to the dormitories of over-excited youngsters. Luckily by Easter, Birmingham Education Authority needed an instructor at Ogwen Cottage Mountain School; I applied and was successful. On 31st August, the end of the academic year, my commuting would end. My condition of employment was that I stopped work immediately if I became pregnant! May that year, 1965, brought not only my favourite month, with cloudless skies and a clean northerly breeze that had sufficient chill in it to walk uphill without sweating, but also our wedding on 21st. I'd always regarded shopping as a necessary evil so I didn't expect my mother to be shocked when I bought the first wedding dress that fitted me. But she was. And my father caught me off guard when we were at the door of the church.

He paused and asked, "Are you sure you don't want to change your mind?"

The future held all that I'd hoped for and my immediate reply was "Nothing ventured....."

With summer came my usual difficulties in breathing because anticyclones brought warm 'good' weather and easterly winds, laden with pollen and pollution from Merseyside; the last thing I wanted was to be outdoors. It was in those final months at the Towers that, probably due to having a base in two places, I was devastated when I discovered that I'd lost my gold watch, a 21st birthday present from my parents. My term was longer than Ron's and to join him in the Alps couldn't come soon enough.

Meanwhile people said, "Isn't this weather wonderful?"

The pressure of a heavy rucksack containing a map, compass, whistle, torch, first aid kit, lunch, emergency food and spare clothing brought itches in places that were difficult to scratch. So on flat, easy ground the rucksack hung from first one shoulder and then the other; wearing waterproofs in warm weather gave me the same problems. But camping was worst of all. Washing in cold water made my finger ends crack and sleeping with sweaty, unwashed skin caused all-night scratching. On return my priority was a bath and the calming steroid creams. But these discomforts came with the package; a return to classroom teaching was not in the remit.

Ogwen Cottage had an interesting history. It had been a staging post for coaches and from the turn of the nineteenth-century its convenient position had attracted climbers to stay. In 1959 three people started to convert a guest house into a mountaineering school, an innovative step because the number of outdoor activity centres could be counted on the fingers of one hand. Trevor Jones told them that the building was for sale, but after one year he returned to his work as an engineer, Ron brought his teaching and technical skills and land agent and mountaineer Tony Mason invested money in the project. Until now most, if not all, mountaineers were predominantly moneyed, professional people. The emergence of highly skilled rock climbers from 'blue collar' workers was in the pupal stage and state educated school children's boundaries extended little further than the sports field.

Ron had begun his teaching career working for Birmingham Education Authority and courses from the authority provided the staple income of Ogwen Cottage Mountain School; the balance came from schools, colleges, youth groups and even from the SAS, Special Air Service. The centre could accommodate thirty students and four permanent resident instructors while the Warden, Tony, lived with his family. The high staff to pupil ratio remained unprecedented for some years.

The competitive, all-bachelor atmosphere created a frequently hard hitting, never vindictive and rarely unkind sense of humour. It was inevitable that a pupil with a stammer would be put in the team of an instructor with the same problem. When the pupil asked if he could f f f f photograph the cat and his colleagues started laughing, the instructor didn't think it f f f funny! After work, at weekends and in the summer evenings, the instructors went climbing, competing with each other to make first ascents of routes of extreme difficulty and their day ended with a pint and female company. It was not unknown for one instructor's girl friend to arrive at the front door while another was being escorted to the back door! Under private ownership Ogwen Cottage Mountain School (often called Og Cot) had influenced and changed the lives of most who had worked there. Young instructors, who had teased, annoyed and insulted local PC Spicer, became teachers and headmasters!

I met Ron before Birmingham Authority decided that it wanted its own centre thereby forcing Ron and Tony to make a big decision.

Ron James, on the right, and Tony Mason.
They owned and ran Ogwen Cottage Mountain School for five years before selling it, as a going concern, to Birmingham Education Authority in 1964.

Their choice was between losing this 'bread and butter' income and to try to keep going or to sell Ogwen Cottage Mountain School to Birmingham as a going concern. They chose the latter. In April 1964, five months before I started work there, they hosted a farewell dinner to thank all instructors and friends who had helped them.

With Birmingham's ownership came many changes. Everyone was very relieved when a big generator, a more powerful source of electricity, arrived; no longer did the last person to go to bed have to run across the car park to switch off our old Lister. But even the new one provided insufficient supply for me to use my wedding present, a washing machine. At least our tiny flat *was* sensibly situated at the opposite end of the building from the dormitories.

Og Cot was situated in a veritable wind funnel where the A5 road was at its highest point, about 1,000ft (305m) and the valley was at its narrowest. Our front door gripped tightly onto one side of the road and Ogwen Lake lapped against the other. When conditions allowed, the downward pointing wing of passing, steeply banked, low-flying jets seemed about to slice through the surface of Lake Ogwen; unsuspecting visitors nearly jumped out of their skins. For city youngsters it must have been another world.

Our only neighbour was the busy Idwal Youth Hostel warden and the nearest pubs were about 5 miles (8km) drive in either direction to very different villages. Capel Curig had attractive cottages dotted along its length and a dramatic open vista to the perfect post card view of the Snowdon massif. Convenient campsites were within easy access of the three hotels' bars, while a youth hostel, climbing shop and cafés catered for the needs of tourists, climbers and walkers. In contrast, throughout the length of Bethesda's main street, shops were wedged in between terraced housing, chapels and churches were on the opposite sides of the road to the pubs but relatively few visitors were tempted to stop.

The nearby mile-long, 1,200ft (366m) deep slate quarry, Bethesda's main source of employment, had been developed in 1771 by Richard Pennant. For some time it was the biggest working slate quarry in the world and an impressive four-poster slate bed, weighing four tons, is a feature today at Penrhyn Castle near Bangor. The need for slate remains but when diamond drills replaced circular saws, whose teeth needed frequent sharpening, a reduction of the workforce was inevitable.

At Og Cot alternate courses were for either boys or girls and all the pupils came from different schools. Most had never left home before, or seen a mountain, so their coach arrived in time for lunch on a Monday, departed on a Friday and they stayed for only one Saturday night. Carol Eaton was appointed to give the girls pre-course briefings in Birmingham, to travel with them, stay throughout the course and, not least, to go with the girls on one-night camps. One instructor could take up to three pupils on a rock climb and ten on walks so they were divided into two groups of six and two of nine. The syllabus included hill walking, skiing on Plas y Brenin's artificial ski mat, a one-night camp, a mountain rescue day. On Sunday morning they went to church.

Instructors and their team took it in turns to cook and serve breakfast and wash up. After morning prayers the hill day started at 1000hrs and ended at about 1600hrs. It was noticeable that both sexes were fitter at the end of the school year than at the beginning and most boys were stronger than the girls. I came to dread walks with girls because their need for frequent rest stops made it impossible to get a

Ogwen Cottage extension in progress

comfortable walking rhythm. But most boys loved a genuine challenge and I enjoyed our longest walk, five Carneddau summits over 3,000ft (914m). Although it often ended with a sprint through Llanfairfechan to catch the bus at 1530hrs, we never left anyone behind. No centre transport was available during the early days after Birmingham took over.

Despite the proverb – one bad apple can spoil the whole crop – serious rowdiness or bad behaviour occurred only in December. Then several schools sent us their mischief makers, we suspected the reason was that they wanted to reduce possible disruption of end of term school Christmas activities. Having safety in numbers, these troublemakers egged each other on and, however hard we tried to tire them during the day, they were able to bounce back at night. Usually I started my holidays exhausted.

Pupils were sent to Og Cot for a variety of reasons: good at sports or non-sporty, over weight, never had a holiday or because they were the hard working, oldest sibling in a large family. Some were unfamiliar with sheets and pillow cases; they had to be taught how to make a bed and I wholeheartedly supported the centre policy, to give social training equal importance with outdoor activities.

Coming from Birmingham it was no surprise that many pupils were from African and Indian families. I felt really sorry for them because, even if born and brought up in the UK, many seemed to suffer more from the cold and wet conditions than those with white skins. Cassius Clay, who became Mohammed Ali in 1964, was in his prime so we used his fame and training image to encourage their efforts. But I suspected that for a few pupils their suffering in winter conditions outweighed the benefits that they gained from the course.

On Sundays Tony Mason took the course to the Church of England service at Llandegai near Bangor. His persuasive skills ensured that everyone attended, even a Jehovah's Witness so that he could make a fair comparison and judgement! Mrs Jones, our small in stature, but large in adaptability cook, from Mynydd Llandegai, had spoken little English before she started work at Og Cot. Tony brought her to work in his Rolls Royce every day. Tony was sorely missed by all the staff when he left, in 1968. Although Mrs Jones was not far from retirement, this determined lady decided to learn to drive. We were thrilled when she passed the test, in English, the second time and from then on she drove to Og Cot in her Mini as though in a Rolls Royce!

Tony was a devout Christian with a unique sense of humour. When we were in the middle of a serious conversation with a Very Important Person – who was straying into pomposity – I found it difficult to keep a straight face. Tony's not always discreet V-shaped finger sign was waving at me from under his arm. Thereby he acquired the name Fingers Mason. His faith and courage, and that of his wife Cecily and family, supported him throughout his battle with Motor Neurone Disease. This tragically brought about his premature death, in 1994, at the age of 63. All who knew him grieved with his wife and family.

After a few years I was becoming bored with the repetitive work, even the permutations of the variables were predictable. We saw different heads every fortnight but after the course ended there was never any feedback - positive, or negative. I suppose it was because I was female, the wife of the Warden, or both, that I got landed with the housekeeper's job. For this I was allowed one day off per course to check stock, order food, cleaning equipment and all other necessities. The perk was occasionally missing the torture of a night out camping or occasionally receiving a set of kitchen knives that came with a dozen tins of soup.

The minus was returning from a wet day on the hill to be greeted by Mrs Jones, saying, "Mrs James, the fish has not arrived."

For some reason no one had thought to ring the shop. From then on I made sure that spare tins of salmon were stocked for these emergencies!

Trying to enthuse the youngsters on yet another bad weather day, when I didn't want to go outside either, became increasingly hard work. During a memorable spell of thirty one continuous days of rain, bogs materialised in new places and I had four pairs of boots in various states of dampness in the drying room. On the worst, monsoon-type day, to beat the weather was impossible. We joined it.

Suitably dressed we organised a very challenging crossing of a nearby river; everyone got soaked and eventually we dashed back for a blissful hot shower. It was safe to walk though the long drainage tunnels above Dolgarrog only after a dry spell. When not even a pinprick of light could be seen at either end, we made it more exciting by saying that there was a hole in the centre of the tunnel floor; for a short distance we all progressed slowly, carefully, sideways with our backs pressed against the wall. Also very popular with our groups was the exciting walk through an interesting old slate mine above Tanygrisiau, Blaenau Ffestiniog.

On a beautiful sunny day in June, visitors would say, "Aren't you lucky to do your sport for work?"

Yes, in that the work helped me to get fit, and in my free time the hills were there to be enjoyed. But I was not doing what I wanted, when I wanted or with whom I wanted to do it.

Winter brought a variety of extreme weather conditions. A gale removed part of the roof of the Midland Association of Mountaineers' hut, at the other end of Lake Ogwen, in 1966. On another occasion a freak rainstorm was so severe that it caused two landslides on the road between us and Bethesda, pinning several cars between them but luckily injuring no one. During this deluge the volume of water pouring down the mountainside brought down a huge boulder from the Devil's Kitchen cliff and streams formed where none had been before. One flowed down the passage at the back of the house, under the door and into the kitchen. Wearing climbing boots, we were busy sweeping water through to the hall and out of the front door when Ron had a good idea. He prised up a couple of floor boards and the water disappeared under the building, presumably to join the river flowing from Lake Ogwen.

While the many extremely cold winters brought ice climbers rushing from cities to battle their way up frozen waterfalls, these extreme conditions brought more hard work for us. Our water supply came direct from the nearby stream. Breaking the river's frozen surface with axes each morning, however, was not as hard as convincing staff in a warm office in Birmingham that the centre, with thirty six people, had no running water for cooking, toilets etc! Rarely were courses cancelled. The instructors hacked holes in the ice and the well-wrapped, excited pupils formed a bucket chain across the car park. In biting winds it was not the staff's idea of the good life, but luckily most pupils found it an exciting adventure.

Only once did the water supply fail in summer. I'd been sitting on the car park wall talking to one of the many well known local characters. Soon after his departure the water supply stopped and upstream we discovered that the lead pipe was not blocked by a stone, it was missing. We left urgent messages for him all around Bethesda; before long he phoned and after he'd denied all knowledge we contacted the police. They found pieces of lead pipe in a scrap yard in Conwy and they brought some for Ron to identify. Of course Ron recognised our grass! When all the pieces were returned to us Ron promptly sold it all - to the local character – and a plastic pipe was installed. Years later, when I mentioned this incident, he blushed!

When I started working at the Towers there were two types of guide, the Rock Climbing guide and the Mountain guide and in 1953 Gwen Moffat became the first female Mountain guide. Although I knew some very talented female rock climbers, women working *full time* as *mountaineering* instructors were a rare species. I made every decision on the hill with safety in mind because I thought that my being female would be blamed should anyone in my group be injured. But with another instructor, a male, I lost the decision-making battle and thereby learned a hard lesson. The ground was snow covered, rock climbing was impossible, so with ice axes, ropes and six students we went up into Cwm Cywion, cwm of the chickens, about an hour's walk away. With warm sun, good snow and clear views the conditions were idyllic. We padded the rocks in the likely landing zones with our rucksacks then we demonstrated ice axe braking, using our body weight to dig the ice axe into the snow to slow and then stop a fall. The girls loved it and it was a delight to see their skills improve. Soon they became adept at rolling over from their back, onto their front, then brake. Once they were happy doing this they had the confidence to correct descending headfirst on their tummies. Competently they dug their ice axe into the snow which made their legs swing around to the safer feet-first descent, then they stopped the fall as they'd done before.

It was after a late lunch that my colleague suggested going further up the cwm to do a roped climb on the head wall. I knew that the time needed to walk further *up* the cwm and to do a route with three pupils did not add up to returning to the centre by 1600hrs. Should anything go wrong, our window of daylight would be short. But he was adamant, I got his renowned, severe 'you're-being-a-weak-female' look and I gave in. The climb took as long as I had feared.

The meal was delayed while the centre was put on standby for a rescue and a worried Ron walked up the hill to look for us. We did get back in daylight. But I knew that many 'experienced' mountaineers, as the newspaper reports always called them, had made the same wrong decision many times before their luck finally ran out. I vowed that never again would I allow myself to be persuaded to do the wrong thing. But keeping this vow wasn't easy.

Chapter 5
Mountain Rescue

Before Ron and Tony bought Ogwen Cottage the lady who lived there had handed out the basic rescue equipment, the Thomas stretcher, sleeping bag and a first aid rucksack, to whichever climber wore boots. However, the official history of rescue in mountains started in 1933 when the Joint Stretcher Committee, after 1946 to be known as the Mountain Rescue Committee, was formed by members of two renowned clubs.

The Fell and Rock Climbing Club, founded in 1906, first published a guide book in 1922 and has been producing definitive guides to Lakeland rock climbing ever since. The prestigious Manchester-based Rucksack Club was founded in 1902. In 1912 they opened their first club hut. In 1945 this club founded the British Mountaineering Council whose role today is 'to protect freedoms and promote interests of climbers, hill walkers and mountaineers'.

Eustace Thomas, born in 1869, was not only a creative, talented engineer based in Manchester, but also he became the first Englishman to climb all the mountains in the Alps above 4000m. Between the wars he designed the Thomas Stretcher. With its strong aluminium frame, canvas bed and pull-out carrying handles, this stalwart stretcher remained in use for over thirty years, only its wooden runners occasionally needed replacing. Eustace Thomas was in good company because, in 1934, Dr Wilson Hey bravely flouted the law and stocked morphine at some rescue posts until, by 1949, the NHS contributed first aid equipment and morphine.

Ron, Tony and the resident instructors became the Ogwen Cottage Rescue Team and it was a tradition that help on rescues came from their climbing friends and nearby mountaineers. It was a busy rescue post and my encounters with the grim results of mountaineers' misjudgements began when Ron and I became partners.

There had been severe weather warnings for a weekend in mid-November and the near freezing rain, falling from early morning, was a sign of things to come. If bad weather was forecast it would arrive, even though the timing might not quite match the forecast, so we decided to go for a lunchtime pint in the Douglas Arms Hotel; its licence had been in the hands of the kind, considerate Davies family since 1913. Here gathered groups of people with a variety of interests including locals, climbers and the RAF rescue team.

By the time we drove back up the Nant Ffrancon valley, the rain was changing to sleet and at Og Cot we heard that three members of a group had not returned to their base, a hut a few miles away. They'd set off to climb a long route on a crag high above the A5 road. Apparently one of them was not feeling well before he started out; conditions deteriorated rapidly and soon gale force winds were blowing the snow into drifts, blocking the road.

After the road was opened the next morning we heard the full story. They had reached the climb and we were told that they had battled up several pitches before deciding to retreat - but not downhill into a valley far from their base! Seemingly determined to return to the Ogwen Valley they'd retraced their steps, uphill, but they couldn't descend the steep path that they'd walked up; they had to walk uphill in order then to descend an easy ridge, in the teeth of the gale. Only when the sick man and his colleague, who'd been supporting him, could go no further did they stop near the main descent path, between the huge mountain wall and the leet (a drainage ditch that crossed the hillside). The third man continued downhill to alert their companions but the blizzard conditions were so severe that they could not find their missing colleagues.

The men were found next day about 10-15 minutes walk from the A5 road. We were testing our new, wooden skis for the first time on an easy snow slope near the road when I was shocked to see two pairs of legs protruding from the back of the Land Rover taking the bodies to Bangor. Ogwen Cottage's hard-climbing and very experienced instructors had not only rescued many climbers but also they had lost close friends in mountains. I listened as they discussed the all too frequent and unnecessary loss of life when mountaineers failed to abort a long-planned goal in favour of an inconvenient, but life-saving, escape route. Their motto was, 'Better to explain your actions to your boss than to St Peter'.

It was a warm summer day when I heard the unforgettably awful thud of a falling body bouncing against rock. I was encouraging first-day-on-the-hills beginners to test the grip of their boots on the first few feet of the Idwal Slabs, easy climbs near Ogwen Cottage and, although I had never heard the sound before, instinct took over. I pushed my group around a corner, away from the rock face, and an attractive young girl landed where we had been standing seconds before. She was unconscious and breathing but sadly had multiple injuries; she died on the way to hospital. That night I could not sleep for wondering what she must have been thinking as she tried to save herself by grabbing climbers' ropes as she fell; she'd slipped, un-roped, above a steep face. Wisely Ron insisted that I led my first rock climb next day.

The resident instuctors accepted that living at a rescue post meant that after a day on the hill they went out again, all too often on a dark, wet night, to rescue the injured. That unmistakeably urgent knock on the door signalled a callout. No pupil on an Ogwen Cottage course was injured during any mountain activity, but in the early 1960s there was no basic training or qualifications available for leaders taking school and college groups on the hill. It was still uncommon to wear waterproof trousers on wet days or crash hats on rock climbs; mountaineers suffered from hypothermia, injury or death all too frequently. However before the end of the 1960s the first courses for teachers and youth leaders (the Mountain Leadership Certificate) and the Mountaineering Instructor's Certificate had been designed and were running. With the hope of international recognition, Ron set up and chaired the North Wales guides' regional organisation in 1964 and by January 1972 a group of guides met officers of the BMC at I. M. Marsh College to review the future of British guiding.

During the five years of Ron and Tony's ownership of Ogwen Cottage Mountain School the full-time professional staff had been available for callouts throughout the year. However, after Birmingham bought it, the staff had school holidays. The first summer, when the instructors were climbing in the Alps and were not available, rescues had been difficult and there was an obvious need to train some helpers. Ron initiated the changes from Ogwen Cottage Mountain Rescue Team to form the Ogwen Valley Mountain Rescue Organisation. He became team leader, Tony Mason was chairman until he left Og Cot, then Dr Cedric Milner took over, and I was the secretary. The enthusiastic volunteers had varied full-time employment and hill experience, most lived nearby but a few were regular weekenders from further afield. Soon we ran training courses for carrying the Thomas stretcher, lowering it down a cliff face vertically with a 'casualty' and then designing ways to lower it horizontally for casualties with spinal injuries. In the early 1960s Ron bought, from abroad, the Perche Barnarde, the Mariner stretchers and the Tragsitz. To find out how best to use them was an interesting exercise; they didn't replace the stalwart Thomas Stretcher, which for ease of carrying uphill had been expertly split into two parts and stiff mesh had replaced the canvas bed.

It was after two tragic accidents that our first aid skills took a stratospheric leap forward. One person had died from a broken nose because at that time 'leave treatment to the rescue team' was general practice and a casualty was lying on his back with blood filling his lungs. Not long afterwards, because the ground was rocky and access with the stretcher was difficult, an injured person was picked up and carried towards the stretcher party. Death was due to severe internal injuries being caused, or compounded, by the untrained lift. Then one man's initiative improved mountain rescue first aid training throughout Britain.

Dr Ieuan Jones was Senior Accident Officer in the Bangor C&A hospital, later replaced by Ysbyty Gwynedd, which received all accident victims. In 1967 he put together a slide lecture that pulled no punches. I loved every minute of his fascinating talks and his challenging sense of humour. We soon learned that the number of puffs on his cigar, on a scale of one to three, would indicate the gory level of the next slide. He showed these pictures, many taken in hospital, in an attempt to accustom us to seeing unpleasant injuries; after three puffs it was not unusual for someone to pass out, often a man with a goatee beard!

Instructor resting 1967

The Perche Barnarde

Passing his basic course theory examination allowed candidates to do first the practical training session and then the very time-consuming individual practical examinations. All were run by Ieuan's wife, Joan, a highly competent, very strict nurse. Ieuan's advanced course was no less compelling thanks to his skilled teaching and the final part was a day spent in casualty. Wearing a white coat I felt the break, saw the x-ray and watched the leg being straightened and finally plastered; this invaluable experience will stay with me for ever.

Soon instructors in other centres in the UK, scout groups and university climbing clubs, heard about Ieuan's course, so those of us who had passed his instructor examinations ran the basic course around the country. Ieuan did more to save lives on mountains, in Britain and abroad, than any person I know. His courage in training lay persons to diagnose and to make decisions on the mountain, often in far from perfect conditions, was unprecedented. Ieuan was a very brave doctor and for many years those unlucky enough to be injured owed him an enormous debt. His hand had guided rescuers throughout the whole of Britain, yet most of the casualties never even knew his name. Sadly Joan died in 1992.

Mountain rescue was not only very much part of our life at Ogwen Cottage, it was also a one-day activity that was enjoyed by our course. Two well anchored pupils, with a rope running behind their backs, slowly synchronised the letting out of their ropes, each of the far ends being attached to a corner of the stretcher bearing the 'injured' person. Matching the speed of the stretcher, a third anchored pupil lowered the rope of the 'jockey', the person who held the bottom of the stretcher away from the rock to prevent it from getting stuck on ledges.

When conditions were suitable, the pupils helped in real searches for missing people because many were needed to look thoroughly in large areas. Our decision to involve our course in the search was rewarded by their pride in being useful, needed and capable of doing so. However people usually went missing in bad weather. In a gale and driving rain, after a casualty had been found, it was impossible to recall the groups in other areas with our low powered mini flares; we were without radios for some years. Then rescues became very much easier when Pye loaned us a radio base set and two portable sets. And after the RAF Rescue service was allowed to evacuate an injured person – they could log the helicopter's assistance as training time - then this blessing dramatically reduced our workload. No longer were vast numbers of hours wasted on searches and the frequency of long-distance stretcher carries, with a heavy patient, dropped dramatically.

Rescue callouts rarely occurred before 1400-1500hrs and they fell into a pattern dictated by the time of year and the weather. When the clocks went back at the end of October, we expected, and usually got, the call to extricate walkers. They had started out late and, rather than turn back while there was still enough daylight to reach the road, they had continued relentlessly uphill, determined to reach their goal. Rock climbers didn't allow enough time to complete a route so they were still on a crag when darkness fell; all too often their head torches were in their rucksacks at the bottom of the cliff.

One rescue however was unique. A man had fallen on Tryfan. Ron was away and I was busy gathering together the kit when another messenger arrived. A man with the same name had fallen on Tryfan so I presumed that the message had been duplicated. By amazing coincidence, two men with the same surname had fallen and were a mere few hundred feet vertically apart. I was very thankful that the time needed to bring the second stretcher did not delay evacuation of the other patient. Because of the stone fall risk, the lower casualty had to be evacuated before the one above could be moved.

Rescues provide exciting mental and physical challenges that bring with them a definite adrenaline kick; this can become as addictive as an athlete's need for exercise. The benefit of having to go out in all weathers was that we rescuers had a very high status with both the press and the police, whose job on the hill was being done for them. But living at a rescue post also meant a substantial, intrusive loss of privacy. We left our outside doors unlocked in the daytime and strangers wandered in to ask a question. Would they do the same in someone's house I wondered? An army officer searched so assiduously for someone to answer his minor query that he found me - in my bathroom! Being woken by knocking on the door in the middle of the night was a relatively rare occurrence but once, when Ron leaned out of the bedroom window, he was asked for an aspirin for a hangover.

His forceful, negative reply was countered sulkily by, "You are a rescue post aren't you?"

I was honoured to have the second certificate for Ieuan's First Aid in Mountain Rescue; Ron had the first. But an unwanted 'first' occurred when a pupil in my class broke a leg on the newly constructed ski mat that snuggled up close to Plas y Brenin. Although forty years ago the suing mentality was in the larval stage, the girl's parents made a claim for this injury. Birmingham Authority's insurance man came to assess the situation and his first question was whether I was qualified. I was!

Being very thorough he asked to see exactly how pupils were introduced to skiing. I showed him the waist-high workbench on which we placed the skis then, wearing their ski boots, the pupils got on the bench and I fitted their boots into the ski's release bindings. The bindings were not called 'safety' bindings because they didn't guarantee to prevent all injuries. The tension of the bindings was adjusted to the weight of each pupil because someone weighing 75kg puts greater force on the system than a 50kg person who wore the same size boot. I was relieved when the inspector told me that I'd done everything possible.

His parting words were, "Parents should accept that to go skiing does indeed carry the risk of injury."

I confirmed this when I broke my leg skiing in Scotland after our fabulous winter spent teaching skiing in Alpbach, Austria. To write his first book, '*Rock Climbing in Wales*', Ron decided that we'd have three month's leave of absence and it was without pay. We'd already passed the Grade 3 British Association of Ski Instructor certificate and to balance finances, we'd look for work instructing in a ski school in the Alps prior to taking our Grade 2 exam.

£50 was the maximum that we could take abroad so, among sheets of paper, we 'hid' £50 notes in envelopes in a suitcase. On Christmas Eve, 1967, we were driving along the eerily deserted autobahns to Austria and after some relaxing skiing we drove to Alpbach early in January. Within two days Ron had work and I started three days later. My only unhappiness was discovering that Ron's pay was 1,320 schillings and mine was 900 – at 72 schillings to the pound! I asked Annilese, an instructor from the village, about this.

She said, "I have the same qualifications as my brother but my pay is less than his."

Equal pay was still well below the horizon!

Ski school work, 1000-1200hrs and 1400-1600hrs, wasn't arduous and the ski school policy, to socialise with our class in the evenings, was no 'hardship'; often our drinks were bought for us. But it was disappointing when, after a careful demonstration of a snow plough, I'd look back up the hill to see all the faces of my class tilted upwards to the sun.

With the arrival of Lent came the reminder that our enjoyable time at Alpbach was soon to end. But not before an ice cave was built on the beginner's slope in preparation for a day of fun. Two instructors tried, unsuccessfully, to 'paddle' a stretcher through a slalom course. Gravity won. Good looking Hansel Bischhofer had learned English from a Birmingham friend and his "Yow Booger" Birmingham-accent voice rang across the ski slopes. Hansel skied wearing a white tent that was supported by an open umbrella and alternately he crouched low then raised the umbrella way above his head. Ron and I 'waltzed' down the slope in a snowplough position. Ron faced downhill holding and guiding me, skiing backwards, until we had to pass through the ice cave. Here schnapps was forced down my throat until it ran down my chin.

Leader training in the Moelwyns.

I soloed ahead to place the runners for an aspirant leader whose second is below and out of sight on this picture.

Despite distractions, we'd worked hard on the book. In it Ron wrote, 'Barbara, my wife, had a hand in every page and in almost every hold, for more than half the routes have been climbed together. Without her drive, both off and on the hills, the routes would not have been finished, whilst the book would have remained an idea'. Before computers, I'd written and rewritten every word in longhand. It was published in 1970.

After a wonderful winter in the friendly village of Alpbach, long walks through heather to small snow-filled hollows high on the Cairngorms were gruelling. Only when the instructors' course was nearly over did an unexpected, late snowfall open all the ski runs in time for the exam day.

We were waiting to be assessed when Frith Finlayson, the head of the ski school, said, "Ski with me."

Our descent was faster than I liked but I was determined to keep up when suddenly Frith turned left into a gulley. Seconds later my ski struck a hidden rock and although I had never broken anything before, I knew immediately that my leg was fractured. Hoping that I was wrong, Ron and Frith did a couple more runs before organising a stretcher. While Ron took the tests, I went in a van first to the doctor in Aviemore and then by ambulance to Inverness. That night we were both sad because he'd just failed the exam.

One of the greatest problems of our residential life at Ogwen Cottage was the lack of mains electricity. The supply line was on the other side of the road but, despite frequent letters, the electricity board maintained that there was insufficient power available for us. So when a few days before we left Ogwen Cottage, in April 1969, the generator was severely injured because the crankshaft exited through the housing, we were thankful that we did not to have to face this problem.

The interesting and busy life at Ogwen Cottage ended when Ron was appointed Principal Lecturer at I. M. Marsh Physical Education College, Liverpool. He would start the three-year Teacher Training Course in Environmental Education. Before accepting the post, Ron confirmed with the Principal that she would consider me for a post of lecturer when the course was established. I dreaded city life and as we drove away from Ogwen Cottage for the last time, many miles had passed before I could stop crying. Soon after we left, Ogwen Cottage was put onto main electricity and a full time housekeeper was appointed.

Chapter 6
A brief exile

We were lucky to find a well built, semi-detached house in Aigburth, a suburb of Liverpool that was a convenient two-minute walk from Ron's college. Although I'd never lived in a city, been without work or felt so fit I tried to be positive about the move because I knew that Ron was looking forward to a change.

However, that I'd miss the ability to step out of my back door and walk off any frustrations on the Glyders was in no doubt. With good exercise in beautiful scenery, I always returned with a feel-good glow of happiness that all was right with the world. My hope, that my career also would progress, was based on the fact that all Ron's students were female and, at his interview, the college principal had told him that I would be considered for a post here, provided my qualifications were suitable. This would be when there were students in all three years and other lecturers had been appointed. In the meantime during this first year Ron had no staff and he needed me to work part-time for which I was paid day rates; any other employment I might find had to be fitted within his dates.

Teaching science and biology in a large 2,000 pupil comprehensive brought new experiences, both plusses and minuses. Laboratory assistants prepared and cleared away apparatus so the pupils could benefit from doing experiments individually or in small groups. But compared to the small, friendly 600-pupil school in Bromborough, it felt like a teaching factory. Another surprise was the divided staffroom, graduates in their degree gowns sat apart from non-graduate teachers. Six weeks there was long enough.

In contrast, work in a small junior school in Speke was both enjoyable and rewarding thanks to the happy, united atmosphere in the staffroom and a good captain running an efficient small ship. When our superb headmaster, Terry Roose, volunteered to take my last class of the day - I needed to go to the education offices before they closed – I understood his staff's one hundred percent loyalty. And in how many schools does a headmaster have to ask teachers to be out of the staffroom by 1800hrs? However, one day in the school's infant department was enough for me: I kept tripping over them!

It was no surprise that I was happiest when I was working outdoors with Ron in Wales, Derbyshire or Cornwall because, unlike school children, his students had chosen to come on the course. The work was not only varied and very rewarding but also the time away from Liverpool passed quickly. The downside was being treated as an outsider when we returned to Wales; a new instructor at Ogwen Cottage gave me a lecture about the good boulder circuit nearby!

But when we were stuck in Liverpool the days were long. Ron left at 0830hrs and returned after the evening meal - my dinner repertoire could not compete with their chef or the cost, only two shillings and six pence (25p)! At Ogwen Cottage I'd become accustomed to enjoying the life of most men, to return from a day's hard work and have a meal presented on the table when I got home. Luckily my childhood list of 'can't do's' had made me the ultimate pragmatist. I ate my evening meals while watching Dougal and the entertaining Magic Roundabout, and looked forward to escaping from the city boredom and pollution during Ron's long five months college holidays.

It was two years later when I applied for a post of lecturer that my hope ended. A letter from the Principal stated 'my decision was made because I do not wish to have a married couple working in the same small department. This may seem old-fashioned to you but I feel quite strongly that this would not be a good thing.' It was a different era, my hopes were shattered and I saw an empty void ahead of me. Mother wondered now if I'd have a child but, much as I would have loved a family, with my inherited allergies and eczema and Ron's dedication to mountaineering, and liking to have a female climbing partner, I decided that the risks were too great.

Ron's full time outdoor education course was unique because this subject usually was allocated limited hours within a PE course timetable. Now I needed a PE diploma. Ron thought it best that I did not go to his college so, in September 1971, I went to Chelsea College, Eastbourne. I dreaded both being away from him and, for free accommodation, having to become an assistant warden and live in a noisy student hostel. The constant loud 'music' was everything I feared, until the three weeks prior to final examinations. Then all was quiet!

In my first term I was just 'getting into' the course when, walking along a flat path, my left knee 'locked'. I was thankful that the operation revealed no cartilage problem; I was told that a piece of fat was stuck in the joint. Another problem was that I lacked transport not only to explore the area but also to get around during my recovery, so my mother gave us one hundred pounds; Ron bought a Mini van and drove it to Eastbourne. Sadly an MOT discovered that it was a rusted, dangerous wreck that I sold, unused, for £50.

I was glad that most lectures were interesting and superb value because I'd calculated my costs per lecture. In only one subject did a member of staff fail to inspire me with a variety of different warm-up exercises, we 'peeled our feet off the floor' at the start of every lesson. But we were expected to prepare an extensive repertoire of warm-up exercises for our teaching practice. However, I didn't want to miss a minute of the modern dance lessons with Olga Napper, a brilliant young lecturer. Her classes never failed to be innovative, fun and worth every penny. With enthusiasm and skill she transformed our very diverse, decidedly motley group into some sort of order, not an easy task. There were eleven of us from places as far away as Canada, Barbados, Singapore and the UK and we had very varied backgrounds and training.

Possibly because all the males of his family had died prematurely, Ron had an impressively high, ingrained level of self-preservation to 'save himself' in every physical sense, not least when rock climbing. He was renowned as a safe climber because, before each move, he made sure that his protection from a fall was as good as it could be. So I was surprised when he phoned me from Scotland to say that he was injured; a student had skied into him, twisting his knee. His clever specialist refused to operate; his knee did recover.

During his recuperation the British Mountaineering Council asked

Dinas Cromlech, Llanberis Pass
Resting during the ascent of Cenotaph Corner,
one of the early female leads.
Photograph by Ron James

him to research the best way to hold a falling leader. The accepted method was for the leader's 'second', who was anchored to the rock face, to have the rope running behind his back, held in both hands; one end of the rope went up to the climber and the other came from the pile at his feet. Provided the leader had used runners, protection to stop a fall to the ground, if he fell he could be saved from serious injury by his companion bringing both hands together while steadily increasing the grip on the rope until it was stopped. We knew the dangers of this method when a friend of ours, Jim, had saved a man's life. A father shouted that he was about to fall off and, realising that the young son could not hold his father's weight, Jim grabbed the rope. He put it behind his back and saved the man from serious injury or worse but Jim suffered damaged kidneys. For his research Ron had designed the tests and he wanted two experienced climbers, me, now back from Eastbourne for Easter, and the famous Joe Brown to be involved.

At Plas y Brenin there was a concrete block weighing 80kg, 12.6 stone – the 'falling leader' – that could be winched up tramlines on an outside wall. Luckily for Joe, I was the first guinea pig. I stood on a ledge five feet above the ground, with the rope behind my back and Ron told me to stop the block above me before it reached the ground. I queried the wisdom of this because the short distance meant that I'd have to do this quickly. We'd been taught always to slow the fall gradually because this would prevent shock-loading both the protection and the person's body. But in the end I did as requested. He released the block, I stopped it and, like a chicken being plucked, the outside of my right knee's ligaments and cartilage were severely torn. Now we were both in the wars. I was already very 'down' because days before this injury, I'd failed to get a job for which I believed my qualifications and experience were well suited, Warden at Kent Education Authority's centre in Llanberis.

Once back in Eastbourne for my third and final term I observed classes until my knee settled down. Now I had time to read Mrs Aubrey le Bond's *True Tales of Mountain Adventure* written in 1906. She'd always set out to climb unknown peaks wearing a long, light walking skirt over the costume. Once away from houses, and before the serious climbing began, she hid her skirt under a rock that could be identified on return.

One of the joys of living at Ogwen Cottage had been that

members of the climbing world called in for a chat. I was thrilled to meet some mountaineers whose pre-war ascents had been achieved with equipment more basic than ours. Their courage and tenacity, strength and technique must have been phenomenal.

Already a member of the ladies only Pinnacle Club, formed in 1921, in 1971 I was honoured to become a member of the Ladies Alpine Club (LAC) that was formed in 1907, fifty years after the 'men only' Alpine Club. The clubs merged in 1975 - after much cogitation, meditation, deliberation and uncertainty! Now I'd been asked to lead an LAC meet in the Dolomites after the course at Eastbourne was over. Confident that I'd be fit, after consultation with Ron, I agreed. I had met some famous female climbers already and among them Nea Morin stood out. She was one of the first ladies to climb alpine routes with another lady and *without a guide* - an innovative, bold move.

I went to London to give LAC members a ten-minute talk about the area and I was relieved to be able to answer all their questions. I couldn't help noticing that most members were of retirement age and some, on the back row, were nodding off, supported on their walking sticks. We had tea and by 1700hrs everyone was leaving and I was disappointed that my time with them was so short when I was scooped up by a wonderful, dynamic lady only a little older than me. Dark haired and slightly erring towards overweight, Heather Wheeler took me in charge. She filled me with sherry in her tiny flat in Elizabeth Street, near Victoria station, gave me a well-wined Italian meal and poured me, happy, into the train to Eastbourne. Her enterprise, energy and unconditional friendship became very special.

We were well into the final term, our exams were approaching fast and I was trying to make up for lost injury time when the timetable included five classes on the link between movement and art. When I entered the room I was bristling with negativity at what I thought would be a waste of time. But again my interest was caught by the outstanding lecturer, Mr Wood, who converted this philistine's approach to art - no mean achievement! For his first practical lesson, he gave each of us six shapes of similar size made of hardboard, I had triangles and another student had ovals. These had to be stuck together to make a sculpture that would be pleasing when looked at from all sides and, to my surprise, this task intrigued me. The time flew by. Our finished creations, sprayed with silver, gold or black, were displayed on a table and it was obvious that some were six shapes stuck together but the successful ones had become one fused piece.

In the next lesson we could split a thin piece of wood into as many parts as we wanted but *all* were to be fixed onto a near-vertical dowel rod that was stuck into a wooden base. When displayed, again these 'sculptures' graphically expressed our personalities. True to form, mine was in parallel lines while an extrovert student's piece was like a star shooting in all directions. I was ashamed of our group and very sad when only two of us arrived for his last lesson, about Picasso, who, Mr Wood said, spanned the time from the picture is a picture to modern art. Understandably he cancelled the class and ever since I have regretted missing his talk. But, thanks to him, I have looked at sculpture and even some modern art with a more open mind - and two of my 'masterpieces' are in my lounge today!

I took all my final examinations very seriously and doing the solo dance was my greatest challenge. I studied meticulously the Valerie Preston Dunlop book until I was sure that I'd incorporated low and high, sudden and sustained and all other types of movements. When she saw it, Olga Napper laughed.

She said, "Your content is fine but why did you travel only in a straight line?"

That's me! I will always be grateful to her for my love of dances as varied as those of Frederick Ashton, Robert North and Stomp.

They say things go in threes and in my last exam it happened. We were on the sports field playing Rounders, a game that traced its roots to baseball and was popular as far back as the sixteenth century. Having hit the ball well, I was running towards the third 'base' to achieve a 'rounder' for my team when a defender got in my way. I dodged her, a ping could be heard by all and I fell to the ground. With my third leg injury in nine months I was now lying there holding my painful right knee, knowing that the medial side was added to the already damaged lateral cartilage. The next day Ron arrived with our loaded car, we drove to the Sella Pass Refugio where we stayed and from here I 'led' my first LAC Dolomite meet with a full-length plaster on my leg.

The average age of these wonderfully competitive and very individual characters among the LAC was sixty. Countess Dorothea

Munich climb, East Face of Tryfan

Gravina had amazingly strong hands and, independent as always, she pitched her tiny tent well away from everyone. Alwine Walford, famous for producing splendid banquets for the Saturday night meal at the Pinnacle Club hut meets, arrived in a mobile home with her husband, Hugo. Nea Morin had lived in France and she had climbed extensively both there and in the UK. Nea's failed hip replacement had left her with a pronounced limp that neither deterred her nor diminished her ability on rock.

She impressed us all when climbing a steep chimney on the nearby Cinque Torri. Unable to do the usual bridging move, a foot on either wall, at one point she had her hands on one side of the chimney and her feet on the other. On another day, to reach the start of the Grade 4, 1800ft (650m) traverse of the five fingers, Funffingerspitzen, Punta Delle Cinque Dita she needed her walking stick to descend nasty scree. But once on rock, she came into her own and climbed superbly. Our last abseil ended near the Demetz Hut and, when the Italians watching realised their age, all the ladies were escorted to the hut and feted with wine.

In September 1975 I was honoured to celebrate her 70th birthday by climbing 'Nea', a route in the Llanberis Pass; she had led the first ascent in 1941. We were four: Nea, her daughter, Denise (Lady Evans) and her son, Chuck. Nea's hip problems neither deterred her nor diminished her climbing ability that still put to shame those half her age. She could assess a hold and know if, or how, it could be used within her limited range of movement. Neither her hand nor foot went hither and thither to test a hold nor did she need a tight rope. What an example she set us all! Nea died in 1986, aged 82. It was a privilege to have met this adventurous, tough and determined generation of climbers and in 1988 Shirley Angel edited *PINNACLE CLUB A History of Women Climbing.*

In the three years that we had lived in Liverpool we had not spent more than two consecutive weeks together in the house. We'd decided to move back to within easy reach of my beloved Welsh mountains when I accepted a part-time job at St Mary's Teacher Training College in Bangor. From Eastbourne, as the song said, 'On the day I went to Bangor', a five-minute viewing was sufficient for me to know that the bungalow that Ron had found, in a quiet, hidden cul-de-sac, was ideal.

With his work mainly in mountain areas, Ron would have little time alone in Liverpool and I was happy to be near friends, the hills and to have work. Half time employment teaching outdoor activities and some PE in the Christian atmosphere of the College was all I'd hoped for. But before then I had to face my second knee operation.

Chapter 7
Home and away

Moving house is near the top of many people's stress tick-list. But in keeping with Ron's single-minded approach to climbing, once we'd agreed the details needed to sell our house we disappeared to the Alps. Good friend, Liverpudlian John Fitzpatrick, a surveyor by profession - but a man with a finger in countless pies - was the ideal person to do the work for us. On return from the holiday I had the knee operation, done by skilled surgeon Robert Jones from Colwyn Bay and watching the Munich Olympics helped me to survive ten days in a residential home in Rhos on Sea. Soon I could walk again the final paperwork was put into both our names and the house was ours. The only minus was a shortage of telephone lines in Bangor; we had to share a party-line with a neighbour.

Coinciding with all this was my father's last illness. Bedridden, his organs were beginning to fail and my mother was running up and down stairs umpteen times a day. Until we moved to Bangor, at the end of October, I was shuttling between Liverpool, my parents in Willaston and my new job at St Mary's College. Luckily a friend in Bangor, Barbara Spark, had a spare room for me. Some years before, she'd gone on an adventurous expedition to the Himalayas with other lady climbers. Now she ran the post-graduate Outdoor Pursuits course at Bangor University. It was a difficult time for more reasons than I could tell anyone and I was very grateful to the head of the PE department, Sylvia Lynn, and her colleague, Ann Dean, for their support in my new work.

My father died in November and on Christmas Eve my mother and I sat near the 'pillow' rocks, a geologist's delight, at the base of Llanddwyn Island. From this idyllic resting place we could see the Snowdonia hills, snow-capped, sparkling in the still, clear cold conditions and, as we talked, their beauty gave some balm to our loss. Here I told her about a memorable day when I'd led 'Dream of White Horses'. I avoided mentioning that Ed Drummond's - he made the first ascent - delightfully named climb near Holyhead, then rated Extremely Severe, was a very exciting traverse along a cliff that dramatically overhung the sea!

After being a golfing widow all her married life I was glad that my mother joined Bromborough golf club. But I was less happy when Ron also decided to play. As always, there were no half measures, so I joined too. Then my mother, whose golf style resembled her hockey-playing days, hit-and-run after the ball, became Ron's mentor in golf etiquette! But I was never comfortable with the chauvinistic atmosphere in the club house. The ladies could not become full members, our annual subscription was less, but when I offered to pay the full amount it was refused; we were regarded by many men as second class members.

The north face Tre Cima de Lavarado

Making 'Rockface', a series of ten BBC television programmes on how to rock climb, was a fascinating experience. John Dobson, the producer from Bristol, read many climbing books and magazines and with impressive speed he'd assimilated the salient facts about our sport. The recordings, on video, were made on rocks near Hathersage and Ilkley because they were conveniently accessible for the huge wagons containing the necessary power sources for the four cameras.

Video's advantage over film was that after a sequence was completed, the tape could be played again on a monitor on site. If mistakes had been made, we could do the action again. John Dobson impressed everyone when courageously, he made a 'Hitchcock' appearance and genuinely did his first ever abseil very competently to camera. He went over the edge of the cliff without hesitation and afterwards presenter John Earle questioned him about nerves.

He replied calmly, "I had confidence in Barbara."

Thank you, John. He helped me to do the index for Ron's book *Rockface* that accompanied the series.

By now I'd led two classic climbs, graded hard very severe plus, in the Llanberis Pass. They were on a dramatic lump of rock, Dinas y Gromlech, usually abbreviated to The Cromlech that stood, like a vertically open book, above a steep scree slope. The well-protected 'Cenotaph Corner', in the 'spine' of the book was a mixture of bridge and balance moves but 'Cemetry Gates', a climb on the vertical right-hand wall was harder. I needed strong arms because hanging from the fingers of one hand, I needed the other to reach upwards and insert a protecting runner. I used my powerful thigh muscles as much as possible to move upwards.

Added to this, as I moved upwards the length and weight of rope behind me increased, making it harder to pull it up and clip into the waiting karabiner above my head. I rested at the holly tree stump before awkward moves led to a tiny belay ledge in an airy, dramatic position 120ft (37m) above my climbing companion, Barbara. Before she started climbing the wind had strengthened, blowing upwards the rope that I'd taken in as she climbed; we were relieved to be off the crag before the weather worsened. The testing of my skill, stamina and mental strength involved in climbs like this enhanced the ordinary things of life. The well-earned pint tasted better and relaxing, tired by physical effort, was a superb feeling. Famous climber Joe Brown had done the first ascent of both these magnificent routes in the early 1950s, getting the idea for their names when he saw a bus with a destination 'Cemetry Gates'. All this was good training for our annual summer Alps trip.

Ron always spent many hours researching the next route that he wanted to climb. To lighten our weight he'd tear a page from a German climbing magazine or photocopy and translate a page from Walter Pause's book *Im extemen fels*, 100 hard climbs in the Alps, that later was published in English. But no amount of fact-finding could give us success on the very long north ridge of Monte Agner. Our goal was to get as high as possible, bivouac for the night and then finish the climb and descend next day; so in the heat of the midday sun we were walking up a dry river bed, full of boulders that reflected and increased the temperature. The long,

On the north face looking down from the Comici route

sweaty, uphill walk in the sticky valley heat was relentless, later, climbing up through downward pointing juniper branches was strenuous and we couldn't get as high as planned. After a sleepless night we'd drunk all our water; we turned back. Most climbers have a risk thermometer and with his priority for safety Ron's temperature reading was low; we never again tried to climb a route of this length.

Our favourite area was the Italian Dolomites with their rolling grass meadows leading up to impressive, huge rock faces; but the Sella Pass attracted me for another reason. The Treaty of Saint-German in 1919 consigned the South Tyrol to Italy and local Austrian traditions prevailed in the Val Gardena. I could assuage my chocoholic weaknesses with mouth-watering chocolate cake, Sachertorte; it originated from Hotel Sacher, Vienna in the late eighteenth-century.

Usually we stayed in Refugio Passo Sella where the owner, Senora Capadozzi, spoke excellent English and always gave us a splendid welcome. From the nearby Demetz hut, where the LAC ladies had been feted, there was a steep slope in both directions. The precipitous, narrow descent challenged skiers because it was squeezed between rock walls. So when one winter the front of my skis touched one wall, turning the *downhill* ski 180^0 was easy. But moving the uphill ski wasn't. Somehow, eventually, I managed to complete the turn. Later these runs were closed due to the number of fatalities.

Another Dolomite speciality was the spectacular Via Ferrata, metal ladder-ways that were maintained by local guides. With minimal technical difficulty, thanks to wire hand rails to clip into, mountaineers could experience dramatic exposed positions that otherwise were the prerogative of Grade V1 rock climbers. When Ron was guiding in the Brenta Dolomites, I soloed the Sentiero delle Bochette. I was enjoying the airy position when I reached a steep, snow filled gulley whose slope not only disappeared from sight hundreds of feet below me but also the hand rail was buried. I crossed with great care! Our evenings here were very special because at the Brenta Hut we had the pleasure and honour of meeting Bruno Detassis, a famous Italian Guide who spoke no English. Ron's good climbing vocabulary enabled them to converse while I chatted with Bruno's wife who's English was excellent.

She impressed me when she said, "I have some trouble understanding old English."

Of all our wonderful experiences in mountains, five climbs were most memorable because on each one I had different reasons to be worried.

When we were discussing the 1800ft (550m) Grade VI Comici route on the Cima Grande de Lavarado, a friend had said that the final traverse was really frightening. Certainly, when I stood looking up at this great face from the path below with Ron and Tony eight years earlier, I never dreamed that I'd climb it. Yet now we were camped in the valley preparing to climb it. The boiled water was in the thermos flask the night before and at 0400hrs it made warm tea that helped us to hastily swallow some stale bread rolls before driving to the route.

It was still dark as we raced to keep ahead of the climbers that we could hear behind us. With just enough light we soloed up the first easy section and at the start of the real difficulties, as quickly as possible, Ron began to climb and only when he'd completed the first pitch did the pair below depart. With no one above us the risk of stone fall - against which crash helmets cannot provide 100% protection – was reduced. With six difficult sections ahead of us, a water bottle each and twelve ginger nut biscuits (they survive best in a rucksack full of climbing gear), rarely did we have a moment to pause, eat or drink.

We were on the very exposed section of the climb when, across the huge vertical face, we noticed two climbers on a parallel, harder route on our left and we began to chat as though we were in a street. It was a truly eerie experience because they were so near yet we knew that if either of us got into trouble neither could help the other. We even discovered that they were Swiss and they knew an English friend who lived and worked in Switzerland.

As the difficulties lessened my arms got more and more tired so the standard felt no easier than the earlier pitches. Added to this I had to keep stopping when my fingers went into spasm. But relief from worry came only when I saw that the final traverse was a narrow, technically easy, very exposed ledge along which, briefly, I crawled along on my hands and knees. We regretted that with daylight disappearing fast there wasn't time to go to the summit and sign the route book; dusk had arrived before we were off the unpleasant slabs. It was late when we reached a bar in the valley where we gulped down the only food they could offer us, soup with alphabet pasta floating in it. In a state of magical, ecstatic exhilaration and exhaustion I hardly tasted it.

Unexpected bad weather gave us a severe fright when, with John Wilkinson, we were on the Grade V 800ft (250m) Cassin route that Ron and Tony had done years before during my first visit. We'd completed the difficult traverse just before the storm reached us and blinding lightning flashes were enhanced by the blackness of the clouds all around. Quickly, but careful not to drop anything, we stripped ourselves of all the metal climbing equipment and hung it down inside a huge flake of rock that was partially detached from the main wall.

Then we put on waterproofs and stood with backs against the wall, feet on the top of the flake, like three budgies on a perch, hoping that our position was safe from a lightening strike. Our car was parked near the hut and when a bolt of lightening struck nearby, the ground became incandescent. I looked away and, after what seemed like ages, I glanced back. The area was still glowing fiercely. It was a relief to find that the car and the hut were undamaged. But a huge boulder nearby had been split, scorch marks were all around and an acrid smell was still there.

It was on the 1150ft (350m) Grade V1- Schusselkarspitze that I had to cope with a serious problem of our causing. To abseil down, the two different coloured ropes were knotted together and one was threaded through the anchor point; afterwards we pulled down the rope with the knot! As always, Ron had descended first because he was experienced in finding the next abseil peg, leaving me on a tiny ledge feeling decidedly lonely. He was out of sight; communication was difficult, bordering on impossible, when I noticed that the knot was beginning to unravel. Immediately I grabbed tight hold of the rope ends.

I knew that he'd reached the stance when the ropes went slack. To stop them from getting stuck when we pulled them down after I'd abseiled, I knew that the next thing he'd do was untwist them, 'skipping rope' fashion, until they were parallel. I screamed at him to leave the ropes alone and eventually he understood. Carefully I hauled up two heavy ropes, took the weight off the errant knot and re-tied it without dropping either rope. Only then could I abseil down to join him.

Only one abseil, on the 240m, 787ft, Grade VI the Petit Clocher du Portalet frightened me when thinking about it afterwards. The obvious crack rose diagonally leftwards up the steep face and to protect climbers from a pendulum swing, at regular intervals huge wooden wedges had been jammed into it. Feeling amazingly safe in this airy position, I'd enjoyed every minute of the climb and when at the top of the abseil I was glad to see that it ended not on a tiny airy ledge but on terra firma. This time I went first.

As I descended I realised just how truly knife-edged the ridge was. There was a massive steep rock face both to my left and right and it was vital that I didn't pendulum either way. I was literally 'au cheval' with a leg on each side of the ridge in order to prevent myself from swinging onto either face. If I had done so I'd neither have got back to the ridge nor had sufficient strength to climb up the rope. Never had the ground felt as good, as I clutched the ropes tightly while Ron descended. Later, as we relaxed in the doorway of the Cabin d'Ornay, all our challenges were put into perspective. On the hut guardian's radio we listened to Neil Armstrong describing his exciting first steps for mankind!

Only one climb, the Grade V1 north face of Furchetta, was done after a heavy night's drinking and very little sleep. It all started at Innsbruck station's bar where we'd arranged to meet friends from Wales. Round after round of beer was drunk as, throughout the hot afternoon, they arrived to join us. By early evening hunger forced a decidedly unsteady group to stagger to the Maria Teresien Strasse for a meal - and more drinks! Ron wanted to stay, to see who ended up with whom, but settled weather was the only time to venture onto hard routes, the forecast was good and I won.

Before we'd reached the outskirts of Innsbruck it was obvious that Ron was in no state to drive. I had drunk little, so I thought, and I drove up the Brenner Pass to the Italian frontier with a near horizontal husband going, 'Hic, hic' in the passenger seat, to the amusement of the customs officer. About two hours later, in Vilnostal, we blew up our airbeds and by 0200hrs we were asleep beside the car. But four hours later, as I rolled up the air bed, an overpowering smell of beer fumes hit me. We carried our heavy rucksacks up steep, unpleasant scree, a mass of small ball bearing-like pebbles and I had another new experience, to taste beer in my sweat! To save Ron's arm strength I had the second rope in my rucksack until we reached the main difficulties. The hardest part, the crux, was a chimney 'blocked' by a huge chock stone, above which was the route book. In it he wrote the date and our names. Then he shouted down to tell me that the week before the first lady to climb it was with a local climber, the famous Reinholt Messner, but we'd made the first British ascent.

Only as we finished the climb could we see that a storm was approaching, fast. Still decorated with slings and karabiners, an exhausting run/walk got us to the hut, just, as raindrops the size of dinner plates began to fall. The room was crowded with smartly dressed Germans who'd walked up from the valley to spend a night in a hut and we feared that there'd be no bed for us. At first the guardian didn't believe that we'd done the route. Only after we'd answered his discreet questions, about the chock stone, we were well wined and dined and even spared a night in a dormitory. We slept well in a quieter double room.

Back home I'd been at St Mary's College only two years when we heard that it would close. The contraceptive pill was blamed for the reduction in the number of pupils and there was a nationwide pruning of teacher training colleges. St Mary's would amalgamate with the University, but only a few staff could be employed. Realising that I needed a degree I enrolled in a part-time Bachelor of Education (BEd) course in Bangor.

A year later Ron was worried about his new, one-year diploma course for teachers starting in September so, for the first time ever, we returned home early from the Alps. Then disaster struck. Two lecturers in Ron's department were killed in an avalanche, leaving their wives, each with one son, waiting for them in a campsite in Chamonix. The appalling shock and traumatic time for all was compounded when one man's body, buried in the avalanche, was not found. Without it, the problems in obtaining a death certificate, and thereby starting probate proceedings, were considerable. For Ron, to the terrible sadness at losing colleagues was added the predicament of a department short of staff.

It was soon after his term had started in September that I sensed something was wrong and I presumed the cause was his new course. But before the term ended I learned the full meaning of 'the ground taken from under your feet'. I was traumatised when Ron left to live with a teacher on his new course.

Chapter 8

Adaptation and job seeking

Although my loneliness was overpowering I had to put on a brave face to save my mother from further distress. Evenings were the worst. By about nine o'clock I could stay in no longer but I felt that I daren't visit anyone twice in one week. Everyone was occupied with their family, their work and their own recreation time. I got offers to come round any time which seemed very similar to telling a drowning person that there was a lifebelt over there, swim for it. I needed one to be handed to me.

This nightmare year of emptiness, compounded by worry about finances, was not helped when a good friend said, "Divorce is six of one and half a dozen of the other."

I believed, rightly or wrongly, that while friends gave the bereaved sympathetic support, being divorced made many fearful of 'taking sides'.

When you are down everything seems to go wrong, even my good golf shots managed to hit a rock and ricochet into a gorse bush! Luckily I soon realised that to find a job I needed a good degree more than ever before. I stopped taking the sleeping pills and concentrated on my BEd thesis. At nearly forty, I had no job and to keep my home I was in urgent need of a salary so that I could get a mortgage.

The best thing in all this was that Ron, having learned from his previous divorce, said that we must keep talking; if we didn't, only the solicitors would benefit. I knew that it was vital for our friends to know that the three of us could be in the same room without being at each other's throats. We were right. When Ron read to me my solicitor's letter, the facts were accurate but their presentation was aggressive. Had we not talked, the polarity between us would have been irreversible. Eventually friends realised that we were still talking while acquaintances thought this weird.

In 1976 I received my Honours degree, Bachelor of Education 2:1, the divorce became absolute and I was on the dole when made redundant by the closure of St Mary's College – a memorable year! That summer the weather was perfect and I ached to be climbing on dry rock, so I went to Clogwyn du'r Arddu, a crag high on Snowdon that was rarely in condition, in search of a climbing partner. There could have been no kinder person to share what was to be my memorable last day climbing on 'Cloggy' than Paul Nunn, guide book author and one of the nicest men in the climbing world. I also did some great climbs, including The Grooves, on the shady, usually wetter side of Llanberis Pass, with Ron and his new partner, Ginny; I came third to retrieve his runners. I was hanging on to a way of life that I knew had gone for ever and I doubted that I'd climb again in the Dolomites.

The divorce law then had a rule of threes. If a Principal Lecturer salary was about £6,000 and my teacher's pay was £3,000 per annum, the two were added together, divided by three and my salary deducted from the total! I would have no financial help. I stopped eating expensive meat while keeping one luxury; every evening I had a small glass of cream sherry that became two and then three. Jobless and with my morale at rock bottom, a spiral into more problems was saved by the help and encouragement of friends in the climbing world and in the RAF. Eventually I saw, in the *Times Educational Supplement,* an advertisement for a temporary Burnham Lecturer with the Ministry of Defence to train young soldiers in Folkestone; I was successful.

In January 1977, I closed down my home in Bangor and began my journey south in an overloaded Mini. A mere two hours into the drive, in Llangollen, it broke down but mercifully the points were quickly replaced by the garage man. The M25 had not been built and when I arrived in central London in the rush hour, I couldn't see any signs to a bridge across the Thames. It was a nightmare but somehow I found the A20 and by the time I got to Folkestone, snow was falling. I saw 'Inf. Jnr Ldr Bn', but I needed a translator; it was Infantry Junior Leaders

Battalion, IJLB. Without a map, guidebook or interpreter, I had landed in what felt like, and was, a strange country with another language.

There was no time to think of the past. I needed 100% concentration to survive whatever came next. My only briefing was to call the officers by their Christian names, the rest by their rank – and the Officers' Mess was at the farthest corner of Shorncliffe camp from the Sergeants Mess! I'd barely found my way around when, after three nights in a bed and breakfast, I was sent for six weeks to teach skiing in the Cairngorms. With my rucksack and my skis at 0400hrs I waited on a bitterly cold, crowded-with-soldiers Folkestone station platform for our troop train that finally departed at 0640hrs. I had learned my first army phrase 'rush to wait'!

Freezing cold and knowing no one, I huddled into my sheepskin coat and scratched away the frost on the inside of the window. The train had been overnight in a siding and two unpleasant hours passed before the heating was switched on. On arrival at Crewe station the packed lunches that were lost were found, and this long, tedious and tiring journey taught me a lesson, never, ever, travel without a good supply of food and drink! What an introduction - but it wasn't over yet!

Infantry Junior Leaders Battalion Plaque

It was 2300hrs when finally we arrived at Cameron Barracks, Inverness, where I was greeted with the news that my arrival was unexpected; apparently no one had informed them. It was too late to find a hotel open. Fortified by some hot soup I was looking forward to a warm bath and bed when they sprung another surprise on me. We were ordered to fit the young soldiers with their ski boots. It was 0130hrs before, after a quick wash of my face and hands in the officers' washroom, I was offered a damp bed in an alcove of an office. Here I slept curled up in my sheepskin jacket.

By 0630hrs we'd breakfasted and were on the snow-covered parade ground where we fitted the soldiers' ski boots to their skis before departing in coaches to the Aviemore ski slopes. On the long bus journey I could relax at last listening to the music of *Copelia*, the choice of Coldstream Guardsman Sgt Burke. He liked ballet and also the fabulous voice of Julie Covington's recently released 'Don't cry for me Argentina'. Appropriate, I thought.

The routine was tough because everything was different. I found myself running on automatic pilot. When the Officer in charge heard that I'd taught *downhill* skiing in an Austrian ski school, he conformed to all the jokes that we'd heard about Army life; he ordered me to teach *cross-country* skiing, something I'd never done! I was shocked that many young soldiers smoked but I put their habit to good use. I synchronised the smoke breaks of my class with another instructor so he could give me advice about ski techniques.

Luckily, after the first week, I was allowed to teach downhill skiing and after one unpleasant evening in a hotel, feeling the odd one out among male travellers, I was found a caravan on the camp. With daytime temperatures around 0°C the metal walls of the caravan lost heat rapidly so the heating was never switched off. Now I could spend more time with my colleagues and things began to improve. I could start to learn about Army life and in the dining room an Officer explained that they ate only after all their men had been served. At Shorncliffe each of the six companies had an Officer with the rank of a Major in charge plus a Non-Commissioned Officer, a Sergeant Major, and within the company each platoon had a Captain, Lieutenant, a Sergeant and Corporals.

The informal atmosphere of outdoor activities, called External Leadership Wing, El Wing, was an ideal introduction to my new life.

External leadership course in Scotland

During a break from skiing, I was amused when Queen's Division Sergeant Barrie Moss, who I believe later achieved the prestigious position of Regimental Sergeant Major, was offering tea or coffee from an urn with a spout at either end. With delight, the young soldiers, usually called 'juniors', stated their preference but the urn was not divided! Catering Corps Captain Cliff Noons, later to become Lt Colonel, was seen performing the skiing equivalent of leapfrog with Sergeant Burke. Cliff joked that anything could be taught in a two-week course. He was right. During my time at Shorncliffe, a charming officer, with no outdoor pursuits experience, was put in charge of the El Wing. After a short course he learned 'on the job'.

After the skiing ended I broke the journey south from Inverness for a recuperative four-day half-term at home before returning to Shorncliffe for another shock. Here with my Education Wing (Ed Wing) colleagues I went for morning coffee to IJLB officer's mess.

A startled subaltern greeted me with, "You're not coming to *live* in this Mess are you?"

No. I had a small, pleasant room in the Garrison Mess nearby. My bedroom was light and airy with a slim partition separating the extremely narrow bed from the sitting area; both had an even narrower window. But I was woken whenever the light switch next door, little more than a foot from my ear, was switched on, prior to water in the other sink gurgling into mine; luckily this room was usually empty.

I was welcomed by a very pleasant group at the Garrison Mess. A charming young, single Lieutenant, Mike Griffin from Wales left soon after I arrived. But Cliff Noons, whose family was in Devon and Trevor Ford, from the Royal Corps of Transport, whose family was in Norfolk, lived here for over a year. It was a tonic to have their good company in the evenings and occasionally we had a fun night out in London to see a show.

I had the rank of Captain, for Mess bill purposes, and immediately I realised that my approach to the wife of the Colonel must be more formal than to the wife of a Captain, while socialising with non-officers was frowned upon. Away from Shorncliffe, the out-of-camp informality of my occasional work with the El Wing was relaxed – only the shouting of numbers on a rock climb, instead of using names, took some getting used to! But from now on my work was in the Ed Wing.

My colleagues were all male Education Corps officers who wore uniforms, or non-uniformed civilians, most of whom were retired majors. I was the first - and I believe the only - civilian female to be employed by the MOD in this teaching role and I was grateful for one good piece of advice, never to throw away any course material. When the Commanding Officer (CO) or Senior Education Officer (SEO) left their replacement would change things – but whatever was changed would be reinstated sometime in the future! This happened.

The Ed Wing syllabus, 'in support of training', was compulsory for all Junior Leaders. 'Juniors' were 16 years old and it was inevitable that their attitudes to returning to a classroom varied. If their platoon staff said that they were wasting their 'bfc' time in that 'bfc' Ed Wing, an enormous attitude wall had to be broken down. It was better when their platoon staff told them to work hard and pass the exams at the end of their year because success could speed their attaining a corporal's stripe and more pay. In 1978[1] Ken Wilson's superb *Classic Rock* was published and if my contribution was read by an Officer or Sergeant they told other members of staff. The result was their more positive attitude towards me and also among the juniors that I taught. These benefits lasted throughout that member of staff's two-year posting to Shorncliffe.

Many juniors had joined the Army either because they had always wanted to be soldiers or because they wanted to get away from an unhappy home life. As boy entrants, they could leave the Army during their first six months, Discharge as of Right (DAOR). If they decided to leave, I hoped that having ironed their own shirts they might respect the work usually done by wives and mothers! Once the DAOR date had passed, they completed the year at Shorncliffe and were committed to a minimum of three years with their battalion.

Some looked very fit and mature whilst others, in an adolescent growth spurt, constantly mislaid their centre of gravity but all were treated the same. Inevitably, after forced route marches ending with an assault course, some juniors suffered stress injuries which ended their army career despite the best efforts of Beth Evans-Smith, the excellent physiotherapist on the camp. The junior leader training was at Oswestry, an ideal rural area, but it had been relocated to Shorncliffe in the

[1] A new edition was published in 2007.

crowded south east where the camp's barracks were better. At the same time the training was halved, to one year - but a quart was still expected to fit into a pint pot!

I was relieved that some teaching subjects - map reading, first aid and some aspects of the leadership course - covered ground familiar to me as did the Communication Skills Course in which the juniors had to give a talk using visual aids. It began with an exemplary Naval Instruction film that would not have gone amiss in teacher training colleges! Our young soldiers, overdosed with hormones, were riveted when in the corner of the screen an attractive dolly-bird in a tight red dress was sitting on a stool, polishing her nails. Gradually her picture increased in size.

Then the man on screen said, "There, you've not been listening to a word I said, Dierdre, come and be introduced."

They would never forget that a class doesn't listen when distracted and will absorb more through their eyes than through their ears. The juniors also practised writing clearly on the chalk board and they learned to make teaching aids for an overhead projector. Their lecture was expected to last 15 minutes. Many did not. I remember only one, about the gory details of work in a funeral parlour, and it ran well over time!

I was struggling to teach two subjects, the theory of weapons and army deployment, their work abroad and in the UK. I even dared to suggest that usually teachers had some knowledge of course material before they taught a class.

But I was dismissed with, "You are a trained teacher, aren't you?" accompanied by that unforgettable 'you're-a-female' look.

Only when I discovered that SAA meant Skill at Arms and that Skill at Arms meant weapons, could I request and get help from QMSI Pat O'Grady.

He proved how rarely he met civilians, in work or outside it, when he said, "I've never met anyone who knows so little about the army."

Bravely he took me to Hythe Ranges, explained how to zero the rifle and I fired the 7.62mm self-loading rifle, SLR, with many eyes upon me.

It was wonderful to learn a new skill from an expert. Thanks to him, at a small range in Shorncliffe camp, the targets soon showed my improved grouping of shots both outdoors, and, with a .22mm conversion, indoors. Watching this professional cleaning the rifle's greasy working parts after every session reminded me of a mother caressing her baby. From then on my zeroed weapon was kept for me in the armoury and my increasing understanding of rifles – breach or muzzleloading - made teaching easier.

Then a member of the Ed Wing staff said, "I've never fired an SLR."

Pat O'Grady ran a course for them until his tour at Shorncliffe ended. I never ceased to admire him and his courage in taking a closely–observed, new female member of staff to fire a rifle for the first time in front of a platoon and staff at Hythe ranges.

But understanding the booklet about Army deployment, UN and NATO wasn't so easily solved. There was no substitute for experience and I had none. So when I heard that Northern Ireland training was happening nearby I requested a visit. One company, *not* in uniform, were the 'civilians' in the very real mock-up village street with shops, a garage and bars. A Sergeant was a window cleaner, I was his apprentice and, as in any street, some 'locals' were in a pub - but with strict orders not to get drunk!

When suddenly a 'bomb' went off, another company came to deal with the incident, to put cordons in place and to empty streets as necessary. When they stood down - military speak for 'the incident had ended' - we went to watch the video. The debrief afterwards impressed me. With strategically placed cameras, mistakes such a civilians being allowed through a cordon couldn't be denied and important lessons were learned.

My first term at Shorncliffe was nearly over when I had a phone call from Ron. He was arranging a ski holiday for 12 people in Courmayeur at Easter, one person had dropped out and did I want to go? If I said no Ron would lose the free place discount and I would lose an opportunity that would never come again. I said yes despite having to share a room with the male technician from a college. No problem. He went his way and I went mine. (My only surprise came when my roommate offered me a 'special' cigarette - made from some herbs that he had grown himself in a greenhouse!) We were very lucky. On our first day the famous Valley Blanche run was opened after a heavy snowfall. The scenery was spectacular, magical, memorable and worth every penny.

Attendance at dinner nights at Shorncliffe was compulsory, but it was no hardship; top class menus cost truckers' pull-in prices. To ensure arrival before the CO a procession of cars passed the guardroom between 1920-27hrs for a meal at 2000hrs. But end-of-meal traditional behaviour was a real eye opener. Subalterns threw Benedicts' mints at each other - many fell into my handbag! The wine flowed, as did the port, but the ladies, (by now Anna, a WRAC officer, had joined the Ed Wing, a WRVS lady and I) dutifully went 'to powder our noses'. Back at the bar, the water siphon and ketchup bottles had been removed, damage prevention by the wise barman, and some heavy drinking and 'games' started. On my first dinner night my SEO was being de-bagged, I was near Colonel Green, the CO, and I suggested a tactical withdrawal.

"You will stay and that's an order," was his prompt reply.

Dinner night 'high jinks' were as well planned as any military campaign could be. Some had become legends. A Mini had been negotiated down the steps and into the hall of the Officers' Mess, whose doors had to be removed to get it out again. Another time on the Mess lawn there were gnomes, lots of gnomes, all in as compromising a position as gnomes can be, to greet the Colonel's arrival for pre-dinner drinks. Next morning the adjutant's phone was red hot with calls from irate householders.

Before the day's work began at 0830hrs, all staff had to read the Battalion Part 1 orders, a list of the day's activities that was sent to all departments. On the day of the annual battalion photograph the officers in one company failed to read them and the CO and staff were kept waiting; the culprits received extra duties! The Ed Wing also had a message book. One memorable missive said, 'Congratulations to Peter on gaining Corps colours in squash'. Added to it was an unsigned comment, 'And congratulations to the rest of the wing for taking his classes while he was away playing squash'. The front cover of one issue of the battalion magazine showed another example of good military humour; a subaltern was reading a book '*On the Psychology of Military Incompetence*' by Norman F. Dixon. And when visiting minor royalty were expected, copious sheets of instructions flew around the camp, including whether she should be addressed as 'Ma'am' as in 'spam' or 'Ma'am' as in 'farm'.

I had been warned that dogs had more rights in an Army Officers'

Mess than the wives did. This was true. They ranged free around the room during the morning coffee break, the dogs not the wives, until a St Bernard joined the Mess. As it circulated, it dribbled into the conveniently positioned coffee cups on low tables; this time complaints were upheld. Less funny was being forcibly knocked off my bicycle by an out-of-control dog.

The owner's explanation was, "Well, he only wants to say hello!"

The funniest argument I overheard was between two dog owners about a very obvious mark on the new Mess curtains. The winner was the owner who pointed out that his dog could not be blamed because of the height of the stain!

Before the end of my second term at Shorncliffe a civilian member of the Ed Wing staff had retired, I was interviewed again and I accepted a permanent post at Shorncliffe. This released me from worrying about mortgage payments for my home in Bangor and repaying my mother the money she'd loaned to pay Ron his share of the house. The 305-mile each way solo drives and a very different learning ladder had left me no time to search for college work within reach of Bangor and nearer to my mother in Willaston. This became my goal.

Chapter 9
Travel

Repeating the same few subjects to different heads every week made the work easy in some respects, but armed with only a folder of information about army deployment I never ceased to dread the class. Relief came thanks to an officer who appreciated my problem. He offered to arrange for me to stay with his battalion in Cyprus during our Christmas holiday and my wonderful mother encouraged me to go by saying that she had my father's sister, Elsie, for company.

I paid all the costs so it was a relief to get a single cheap, £8, seat on an RAF indulgence flight, a system where empty seats on military planes were filled on a last minute basis. I was shocked to find that again my arrival was unexpected. Gallantly they provided dinner that I ate in the corner of the mess kitchen; they apologised that I could not attend their Christmas Dinner and in my bedroom I listened to the band playing. The fun started next day with the once-a-year senior ranks' visit to the Officers' Mess for Christmas drinks. Some serious seasonal spirit hung over the area and it was rumoured that fish in the nearby pond went into hiding!

The battalion spent three of their six months posting in the Dhekelia barracks near Larnaca and I was grateful that they arranged for me to be driven through orange orchards with two Land Rovers and armed escort. During the tour Sgt Attwood explained that these military patrols helped to defend the Greeks; sometimes the Turkish soldiers strayed into their area. The bonus was being able to pick some delicious fruit from their trees.

For the other three months the battalion worked with the United Nations (UN) patrolling the 'green line' that divided Cyprus into the Greek-controlled south and Turkish-controlled north. Different countries were responsible for sections of the line, but they all wore a blue beret and drove white UN Land Rovers bearing the blue UN symbol. A soldier's nationality was unknown, until he spoke. The British UN headquarters, St David's camp, was in an impressive, huge, old box factory and here the soldiers had 'Rest and Recuperation' (R'n'R). The floor was divided into two Messes, a coffee bar and a theatre where a different film was shown nightly. However, groups of about four soldiers lived for up to four weeks in some very basic Observation Posts on the 'green line'. In one OP a soldier had his sleeves rolled up and a recipe book in front of him; he was making shortbread for the first time. Their other duties included accompanying Greek farmers, who needed a special pass when they wanted to cultivate their strip of land parallel to and nearest to the line. To go to the middle strip, the farmers required only a permit and they could cultivate the strip farthest from the line at any time.

On most days I went exploring alone. On a ridge near the Dhekelia Mess, old coins had been found, I set off to explore but before I had gone far a man in Arab dress was following me and it seemed wisest to return. I rented a car and drove to Ayia Napa, where there was one hotel and a deserted beach. I also went to the Troodos Mountains, which were in mist. However, the peace and calm at Stavrouni monastery and the exciting drive up the steep, stony track with very sharp-angled bends, drew me back a second time. Later, when my hire car's wheel hub flew off, I saw that the wheel was minus a nut! An invitation into a Greek house for Turkish coffee and biscuits was unexpected, until I was shown into a room full of tablecloths. I bought nothing because I knew that I'd have to pay for a pocket-emptying scheduled flight back to the UK.

It was after five tough terms that, in my three-week holiday in August, I began to suffer severe chest pains. A friend said that she'd had the same, her dogs had eaten her prescription and she had recovered, so I ignored the pain until it became unbearable. Eventually I was diagnosed with Bornholm's Disease or Devil's Grip, a viral disease spread by faeces of infected individuals that affects the inter-costal muscles in the chest wall and because it wasn't improving, my worried mother came to look after me. Then one night I could hardly breathe; she rang a doctor and an ambulance arrived. It was December before I could return to Shorncliffe, but to feel 100% well took much longer. Only later did I learn that if my heart muscles had been affected I could have died!

Years passed and my many applications for jobs, that were within reach of home, failed. My unhappiness was compounded by the disappearance of the companionable atmosphere in the Garrison Mess when Cliff and Trevor left Shorncliffe. They were replaced by military people who slept here from Monday to Thursday, so from midday on Friday to Monday lunchtimes I rattled around in a huge, empty building. But you're not alone when you're travelling! A weekend visit home filled the time and was possible thanks to my old, gearless bicycle. Whenever I could escape late on a Friday afternoon I pedalled to Folkestone station; the bike went free in the guard's van. Then I had a terrifying rush-hour bike ride, often in the dark, from Charing Cross to Euston station. Provided that I did not miss a connection, the journey took six hours.

Although travelling filled much of my free time, more was needed if I was to achieve my goal, to widen my knowledge of infantry postings. I was delighted when I got a return indulgence flight to Gibraltar. Here the strip was extended into the sea, making the landing an exciting eternity before the engines' reverse thrust took hold – a superb start to a brief, informative 7-day visit! This tiny part of the UK, situated on the coast of Spain, had been British longer than the USA had been united. The military's greatest challenge, after their ceremonial duties were done, was keeping infantrymen fit in such a small area, most of which was filled with a huge lump of rock. Mine was escaping from the persistent 'guides' on my solo day-trip to Tangier to explore the markets. But the most exciting surprise I had was to join a group exploring a cave below the impressive St Michael's Cave. After lowering ourselves hand over hand down a short rope, we inched our way along the minute rock edge inches above a lake. I wondered what would happen if anyone slipped and only at the end did we see a safety boat hidden around a corner.

During a few days in Germany, under strict supervision, I was thrilled to have the riveting experience of trying to keep a huge tank moving in a straight line. But the pinnacle of my unparalleled adventure, for a civilian, happened when I went to Berlin. To my relief this time my arrival at Elizabeth House was expected. Colonel Silvey, the commanding officer of the Education Department in West Berlin, said that he was impressed that a civilian was willing to pay to gain information that would help her to do a better job. This kind, considerate officer arranged for me to be driven slowly along the eerie Berlin wall, to see its manned watch towers and the many crosses where people had tried and failed to escape to the west.

Then Colonel Silvey took me to East Berlin - before the Wall came down! Prior to going through Checkpoint Charlie he showed me the folder of advice available should trouble arise; it stayed beneath our car seat. I understood why. The atmosphere of risk was all around as slowly, under the watchful eyes of many armed guards, we passed through the high-walled chicane into East Berlin. The huge, grey apartment buildings were depressing, but the clever and varied wall paintings were a pleasant surprise. One, a huge, open trouser zip-fastener had in the V a picture of lovely countryside. During our magnificent lunch I was glad that he persuaded me, a non-spirit drinker, to taste genuine Russian vodka. It came in a tiny, frosted, sugar-coated glass and it was superb.

To make the most of my time there, I explored West Berlin using the clean and efficient trains, while being careful *not* to stay in the U-bahn, the underground train, when it continued into East Berlin! Automatic machines were rare in Britain at that time and I was impressed that everyone was honest and bought their tickets at the station entrance. Then I saw why. Four burly inspectors in bright, powder blue jackets stepped into our compartment just before the doors closed and by the next stop they had checked everyone's ticket. Later I saw that a man, about to get on the train, had walked away when he spotted the inspectors. He wandered off down the platform. They followed him. Sadly my train departed then, but I had little doubt about the outcome. The reports of the Pilgrim cricketers' off-pitch activities enlightened me about Berlin's night life!

Other than these few visits, my only escape from the repetitive classroom work was occasional weeks with the El Wing. These started with the dreaded Friday evening drives, hemmed in among the three lanes of traffic going north up the M1 motorway at 70mph. My life was frighteningly, firmly, in others' hands. Once I passed three different accidents, and two bodies, in less than twenty miles; to reach the quieter A5 road at Shrewsbury was always a relief and my arrival at the Tyn y Coed before closing time couldn't come soon enough.

I looked forward to sitting on the bench seat beside a real fire in the Tyn y Coed Hotel in Capel Curig. Here I met two splendid characters, Gwylim's father, Taid Rhos (Taid is Welsh for grandpa) and his friend John Camp (John Hughes) who worked in the army camp a mile away. After their lovely welcome I could relax and unwind before the final, gentle drive down the empty Ogwen Valley road to Bangor. I had thirty six hours at home before clocking up more miles driving to Otterburn, Stirling or elsewhere.

Sleeping in a noisy military camp was unpleasant, evenings in bed and breakfast places were solitary, so once I'd discovered that I could claim allowances for accommodation, I booked into small hotels. During the annual three weeks I worked with the El Wing in the glorious Trossachs in Scotland in May, before the squadrons of midges gathered full force, I became a 'regular' at a tiny hotel in Doune. Here the owner introduced me to Wilma and other great local characters – they all knew their whiskies!

Only in one hotel was I asked to leave. I'd gone into the kitchen to make some tea because at 0800hrs there was no sign of breakfast, transport was collecting me at 0830hrs, but the daughter's mind was on other things. While her mother was away, a farmer's Land Rover was parked outside the hotel. I was allowed to stay – and I never told her mother why I'd entered her kitchen!

Years before a neighbour, Jean Patrick, smiling, had asked, "Barbara, do things always happen to you?" They do.

At Symonds Yat near Bristol the trees, conveniently above and below the rock band, gave us shelter from the gale force wind and good anchor points for the short 'top roping' climbs. Both the climber and his partner who held his rope stood at the bottom of the crag; the rope that joined them was running through a snap link above. The anchor man took in the rope as his companion climbed.

It was all running well when I heard a shout, "The tree's falling down!"

I thought it was a joke, but the repeated shout vibrated with genuine panic, gaps in the soil were appearing, the whole tree was swaying downwards towards the river below; a junior was attached to that tree. I grabbed the climber's rope while another junior, who luckily had a sharp knife, cut free the anchor man and we all moved away. Like a drunken man, the tree swayed until it fell downhill with a crash, smashing all around it as it went. Later a charming officer apologised as he explained that *he* would be writing the incident report!

One day I mentioned to my colleague, Brian Allen, that ever since Dr Cedric Milner's excellent talk, I'd longed to visit St Kilda. Brian had heard about the islands when he was in Sydney, Australia, and he too had dreamed about going there. While playing sports and going on an expedition was regarded as good experience and a useful part of military training, it never occurred to me, a civilian, that I could organise a trip until, in the Garrison Mess, Major Peter Robyns suggested that I took a group there. He had captained the Landing Craft Logistic, LCL, the boat which every summer brought supplies to the military detachment on Hirta, the main island of St Kilda.

If St Kilda was not the most remote outpost of any Army posting, then certainly these islands, situated 41 miles (66km) west of Benbecula in the Outer Hebrides, were the most remote in the UK. Peter told me that in order to test and fire the new generation of missile weapons, in the mid-1950s the Ministry of Defence set up a firing range on Benbecula in the Outer Hebrides. This site was selected because St Kilda's westward position was a suitable base for tracking radars and missile surveillance. In August, when the radar systems were shut down for their annual maintenance, we could visit the island.

With Brian and some juniors we started the sea journey on the LCL at Helensburgh, just north of Glasgow. On our arrival at the quay, there'd been some reluctance to allow me, a female, to travel on the LCL but luckily an empty cabin was found thanks, I suspected, to our CO, Colonel Jon Fleming, of Army on Everest fame! In low mist and poor visibility the LCL inched its way through the excitingly narrow Sound of Harris and with perfect timing the visibility improved as we approached the dramatic cliffs of Stac Lee, Stac an Armin and Hirta.

The daylight was nearly gone when transport was found to take us uphill to the tracking station from where we walked to the top of

Conachair, 1397ft (426m). Never before had I kept a hand above my head to avoid injury from the dive bombing skuas; I lowered it when the bird was close. To sit on a cliff edge communing with gliding fulmars and gannets was a magical, if brief, experience. The tide dictated our departure and in the dusk we descended to the twinkling lights of the military settlement. We'd had three spellbinding hours on land.

The following year I was not allowed to travel with my group on the LCL. Unwilling to miss the visit I'd organised, I combed the western isles for a boat to take me and in doing so I visited many of South Uist's beautiful islands. On Barra, the scheduled plane landed daily on the beach but its timetable matched the tide. Eriskay and Vartersay looked idyllic in superb sunny weather. Too late, on Bernaray I found fisherman Kenny who could have taken me. But it was third time lucky. Arriving in a boat from Oban we stayed for ten magical days on Hirta. My group slept in the military camp; I shared one of the 'old' cottages with a mouse. When I heard that mice had chewed through a TV cable and stopped reception, I made sure that they were too well fed to jump onto my bed while I was sleeping!

On the advice of the nature reserve warden, Wally Wright, I enjoyed our early morning patrols to catch young Puffins hiding behind oil drums; we threw them into the sea where they were safe from preying birds. Perhaps our most dangerous walk was negotiating the potentially leg-breaking puffins' burrows on the (now separated from Hirta) island of Dun. On a bad weather day the cooks taught us to make bread for which I am very grateful (I've made my own ever since). But our on-going project was making our St Kildan mail boat. It had been a means of communication for the island's inhabitants. Into hollowed-out pieces of driftwood we put two stamped post cards, one to ourselves and one to the military on St Kilda who kept a record of all mail boat landings. A plastic bottle was attached to our driftwood – the St Kildans had used birds' bladders for the float – and when the wind and tide were right we 'posted' the mail boats into the sea. Mine was found on a beach on Sanday Island in the Orkneys - but that's another story!

In the evenings the juniors learned more about military humour. One night the major and I became Egon Ronay assessors of the best pub-bars; they were set up in several cottages. The winner was the Sergeant in charge of the first aid centre. His customers were provided with crutches when leg-less, eye patches when blind drunk, a bed when unconscious and they could - and one man did - drink and swallow at the same time thanks to a nasal tube from a bag containing beer! Once the winter storms had removed the sand on the beach, the LCL couldn't bring supplies; they had to be helicopter air-dropped. On this lonely outpost, a major dined alone, and the 30 technical staff, cooks and the Sergeant ate together.

The sad story of the St Kildans remains an indictment upon society. The last inhabitants asked to be taken off Hirta in 1930. All sixteen houses were left with a Bible on the table and a fire in the grate – as it had been for about a thousand years. In the company of kind boatman Kenny, in the swell left by a force 8 gale, I was sad to say goodbye to this unique place. In July 2005 St Kilda was awarded Dual World Heritage Site Status for both natural and cultural significance. It shares this honour with wonders such as the Historic Sanctuary of Machu Picchu in Peru. My group returned to the mainland on the LCL!

1983 was without doubt my most memorable year. My brain cells were at serious risk of atrophy so in January I started a fascinating, third level, half-unit Open University course called 'The Changing Experience of Women', recommended by friend Phil Scraton. (It was thanks to Phil and Sheila Scraton and the Merseyside Mountaineering Club that I'd had some magical weeks climbing on Lundy Island, managed by the Landmark Trust, in the Bristol Channel.) My first essay, to compare and contrast two advertisements, caught my interest. The one for soap showed a near naked lady, bath towelled, looking out of the window at her man returning from skiing, while for a stereo system a tight, shiny-cat-suited lady was standing with arms on her hips and legs wide apart.

I was enjoying the course when I had a succession of unpleasant shocks. I was the longest living-in member of the Garrison Mess and I received the message that as a female I was no longer welcome there. My SEO made enquiries and reported that the situation was non-negotiable. After much rushing around I signed the papers to buy a tiny, 26ft square, semi-detached bungalow before leaving for the Easter holiday. As always, en route to Bangor I called to see my mother and I was shocked to see her condition. A packed bag was in the porch awaiting my arrival and after the grim weekend my clever GP immediately recognised her problem, temporal arteritis, an inflammation of the arteries of her head, for which she needed steroids.

I returned to work a week late, tortured with the knowledge that she should not be left alone. I'd been back at Shorncliffe for only two weeks when, returning from a Sunday taking the juniors climbing, I was greeted at the Guard room with more devastating news. My aunt Elsie, my father's only sister, had been found dead in her chair. I cried throughout the train journey north. Mother was too ill to help and after the Whit Monday holiday I had four working days to clear her two rented rooms. I filled mother's house and a neighbour's garage before returning to Folkestone. What a five months!

The only good thing to happen in 1983 was that in May a skin specialist in Folkestone ordered me to come off the 5mg per day Prednisolone pills that I'd been taking for nearly fifteen years.

From now on my mother's brave battle with deteriorating health was a constant worry. My support and advice came from Joyce Tait, the welfare lady on camp. She stemmed my tears with kindness, coffee and comforting words given unstintingly however much work was on her desk. My commuting life, between Folkestone, Willaston, Bangor and El wing work, was wearing me down and my eczema worsened with the stress. I had never felt more alone. Desperate to be near my mother I did year four of a fascinating Road Safety Officer's course at Middlesex Polytechnic and became a member of the Institute of Advance Motorists before I realised that without speaking Welsh my job prospects were negligible.

In 1986 my mother tripped in her garden in the dark and broke her hip. She was lucky that her neighbour heard her weakening calls for help. From then on I was torn apart by her desperate phone calls. Her long-term, large doses of steroid for the temporal arteritis caused her severe back pain and there were days when she had to crawl to the toilet. After an exhausting, arduous preparation of a fresh meat and vegetable meal she was wheeling her trolley to the table when it caught on a ridge between the kitchen and the lounge; her meal fell onto the carpet but bravely she struggled on until the following year.

I returned home in mid-August. Her kitchen cupboards were empty. She could neither cook nor look after herself and the doctor warned me not to hope for any improvement. Courageously she said

St Kilda

(Above) Baby puffin being thrown into the sea to save it from Black Back Gulls.

that a nursing home was the only option and she faced this grim fact with fortitude. On 12th September 1987 she left her bungalow. The short journey was terrible for her – she never glanced back - and I was with her all the way.

I could empty her home only in short spells before I was emotionally drained. I will never cease to be grateful to Sam Evans from Newborough who had done some gardening for me. With his help and strength we emptied her house and filled my garage. I carried the burden of knowing that she had needed my help long before then. The years of commuting and stress, dreading what the next phone call would bring, demolished my health and I never went back to work. I was thankful to support her. When I realised that other residents wandered into her room and tried to use her commode, I found her an excellent nursing home near Conwy, run by the wonderfully caring Ann Bithell. The relaxing sound of ducks and hens below her window brought back memories of our family home in Willaston.

Chapter 10

Retirement

Seeing my mother's health deteriorating was hard to bear and yet again I'd longed for a brother or sister. I was in desperate need of mental diversion: I'd never achieved fluency in any language and I decided to give learning the Welsh language my best shot.

The five days a week for eleven weeks Wlpan course (Wlpan is a Hebrew word for the intensive course for immigrants in Israel) was superb. It bore no resemblance to chanting verb conjugations as we'd done at school. Our dynamic teacher, Elwyn Hughes, infected me with his enthusiasm and from his first lesson we spoke Welsh. By the end of a two-week summer school in July - it followed the Wlpan course - I was near to tipping over from learner to speaker. But sadly after the holidays I needed a more intensive course than the two hours one morning a week session; my fragile Welsh language skills were overwhelmed when I learned to fly a plane.

As a much needed long-term investment I intended to rent my tiny bungalow in Folkestone, but a succession of estate agents let me down. I had to remind one to renew the tenant's contract. Another didn't notice that a lovely little folding chair was missing and that a huge double bed had arrived in the front room (I paid to have it removed). After one tenant had left, a £400 phone bill on the mat greeted my arrival to check the place! I could take no more and at the lowest point in the housing market, regretfully, I sold my bungalow at auction. The price covered my mortgage, just.

Coinciding with all this was the stress of emptying my mother's house; the Folkestone years took their toll and nothing but problems seemed to surround me. Mother's doctor had told me that she wouldn't get better and he advised me to have a much needed break, now rather than later. Needing somewhere different, but without language barriers and package tours, I remembered the military video of the Falklands conflict. I went to the Falkland Islands (FI) Government Office in London where I received all the help and advice that I needed. Thankful that friends would visit my mother, I paid, exactly a month prior to departure, the £1000 for the flight and booked accommodation for the first three, out of six, weeks. The rest I'd sort out when there.

I dreaded the long journey but I was flying with the best airline in the world, the RAF. At Brize Norton I was grateful to have a bath prior to the 2200hrs departure. With surprising speed the night ended and early on Friday 16th December 1988 we were landing on Ascension Island; we were half way there. We felt like royalty as we walked between lines of military personnel to a fenced outdoor area where we were locked in - to prevent us from wandering off and delaying departure! We could sit at tables in the fresh, warm air, help ourselves to the urns of free orange or lime juice and by the shop there were toilets, huge wash basins and lots of hot running water.

The end of our second eight-hour flight was near and I was beginning to wilt when we were told to look out of the plane window. A Hercules aircraft came nearer and nearer; I took photograph after photograph until it was close enough to see the pilot's face. It was only five years since the conflict and the Tristar's approach to Mount Pleasant Airport broke radar cover, hence the reason for our escort. After landing at 1330hrs, Stanley time, we had to stand for a long and detailed briefing about landmines, their appearance and how to avoid them. Exhausted, all I remembered was that well-signed fenced areas must be avoided before we were taken on the last leg of the journey, a 30 miles, one hour drive on the extremely rough, stony road to Kevin Donnolly's accommodation in Stanley. (Today, tarmac only tops and tails this road.)

Thanks to the UK being five hours ahead, next morning I was ready when Graham Bound from the FI tourist office came to collect me at 0810hrs. The sea was too rough for us to travel the 15 miles to see the king penguins on Volunteer Point. We diverted to the nearer

The Falkland Islands 1988
(Above) The Tristar broke the radar cover as it approached Mount Pleasant Airport so we had an escort on each wing.
(Below) Pebble Island

Kidney Island where we walked through the head-high tussock grass to a magical experience, sitting within touching distance of the appealing rock hopper penguins. They ignored us as they made their laborious ascent from the sea to their nest. What an introduction!

About 300 miles (483km) from Argentina, the Falkland archipelago's land area, 4,700 sq miles, consisted of two large islands, East and West Falkland, over 700 smaller ones and a highest point only 2312ft (705m). Leaving Stanley airport at 0815hrs next day, stunning views from the air and wonderful small field landings later, we landed on Pebble Island which is about 24 miles long and 5 miles wide. At the Lodge the warden, John Reid, introduced me to a BBC TV crew who were going to recce the whereabouts of sea lions, Magellan penguins, a red buzzard and a peregrine falcon. I accepted their offer of a lift.

They left me by a perfect, white, diamond–sharp sparkling beach. Here I sat, alone, fascinated by the line of Gentoo penguins marching, or paddling on their tummies, to the sea. It was hard to tear myself away to explore and really 'get the feel' of the place, but soon my mood changed. I stumbled on the monument to 'HMS Coventry', a destroyer hit by two bombs. It sank within 15 minutes with the loss of 19 British sailors' lives. This incident undermined confidence in the strategy and tactics of the British navy and led to significant changes in the naval approach to attacks from the air.

Next day I was descending Marble Mountain when on the horizon I saw a Land Rover. Had it been horsemen it would have been an ideal setting for a Clint Eastwood film - lone stranger meets locals in a barren landscape! 'It is a small world' applied even 8,000 miles from home. Curious to see a solo walker the driver stopped; we introduced ourselves and found that we knew people in common. Penny Bollinger had lived in North Wales and knew Pete Douglas and other members of the Ogwen Valley Mountain Rescue Organisation! Penny, a 'travelling' teacher, stayed in 'campo', a Spanish word meaning countryside, for three weeks with families who had children under eleven. Secondary age children went to school in Stanley where they stayed from Monday to Friday. Later I met Penny's teacher friend, Sara; the Principal of Ron's college was a close friend of Sara's family! At Fox Bay a lady from Bangor University showed me the first fish farm in the Falklands and my hosts that night were Mainnh and Steve Howlett.

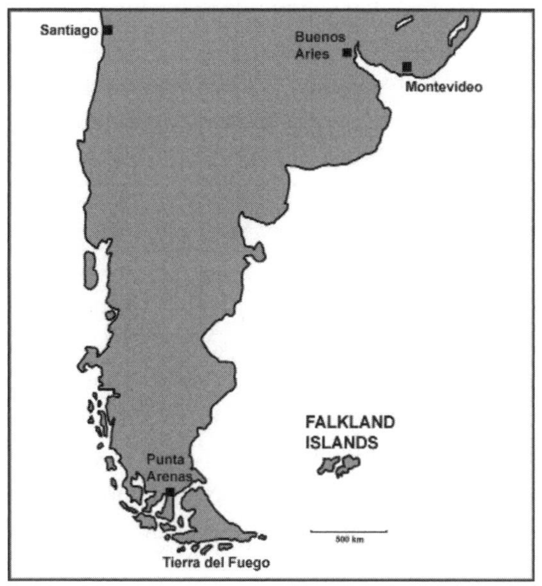

South Atlantic

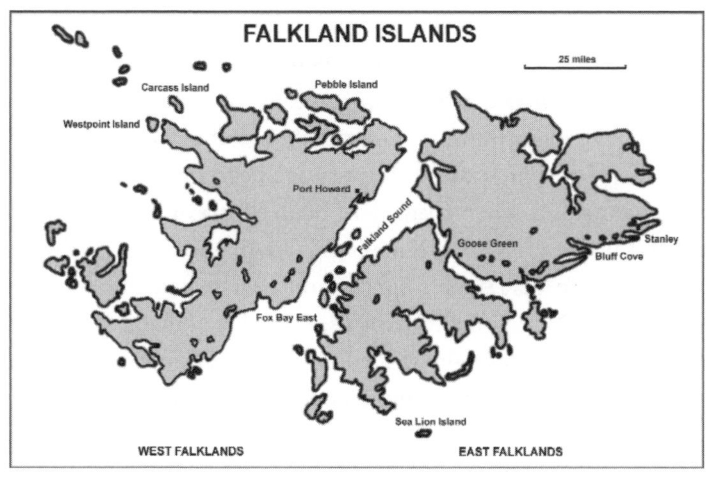

Falkland Islands

Thanks to Ron James for his help in making these maps.

Steve was an ex-boyfriend of Cathy Edwards whose parents, Robin and Audrey, lived next door to my family home in Willaston!

Before my return to Stanley for Christmas, during one whisky-laced evening, John Reid advised me to visit Eileen Vidal in the tiny radio shack in Stanley. She would contact people in the 'campo' and arrange for me stay with them. I did. A very busy Eileen told me to return with my plan after the New Year when the celebrations were over.

By now I'd been travelling for eleven days and it was a relief to be settled in one place. The weather had changed from a steady Force 4 wind with clear skies and sunshine to cloudy and chilly when my RAF friend and his colleagues came from Mount Pleasant. Chatting non-stop they drove me to Moody Brook, a sombre place with evidence of war all around. What a contrast to the mood of optimism and hope that was evident that evening at the carol service held outside Stanley's Christ Church Cathedral!

On Christmas Eve I decided to walk up Tumbledown and I was glad that my friend had given me some maps. With no paths I laughed at myself as I skirted around not only the obvious minefields that were surrounded with skull and cross bone flags fluttering in the breeze but also the bomb craters. I was near the summit when I spotted some very threatening black storm clouds approaching, fast. Just in time my waterproofs were on and I was crouched by a boulder beneath an old umbrella that went with me everywhere. As the squall battered me on this barren, desolate hillside, I remembered the videos I'd seen at Shorncliffe. How much worse it must have been for our soldiers. What did surprise me was when chatting to Euan Morrison, the proud owner of a stone house (many were made of wood) and some of the other locals, to be told that there might be oil near the Islands. Could this have been why the conflict took place? Later I read that it was not until 1998 that six test wells were drilled and only traces were found; later the hunt was resumed, two miles below the sea bed.

The claim to fame of the racecourse near Stanley was that in September 1966 a DC 4 plane had landed and some time later it had successfully taken off. The course lay dormant until Boxing Day when my friend planned to take me to the first of three days' horse racing. As I waited for him and his companions - they never turned up - I was

Capel Curig
The Snowdon horseshoe with Plas y Brenin in the foreground.

Llanddwyn beach, Anglesey

Ogwen Valley Mountain Rescue Organisation
Dr Cedric Milner, Chairman of Ogwen Valley Mountain Rescue Organisation, guides the Mariner stretcher lower during a team practice.

On Clogwyn du'r Arddu in the early 1960s
Climbing Shrike, then graded extremely severe, a steep, strenuous route with good holds. The route was named after a bird that impales its prey on spikes in order to tear off the flesh.

Relaxing after a memorable climb

When Nea Morin led the first ascent of the route in 1941 she named the climb Nea. It was graded severe and in September 1975, soon after her 70th birthday, she repeated the climb in perfect style.
Later the route was altered by a rock fall.

Finals to land at Naples Airport

I took the photograph with a Rollei 35 camera.

St Kilda

Village Bay with Boreray in the distance.

Falkland Islands

Inter island transport is by the Islander plane.
For weight and balance calculations the pilot requires passengers to stand on a weigh scale prior to take off.

El Teide

El Teide National Park both impresses visitors and attracts scientists from all over the world.

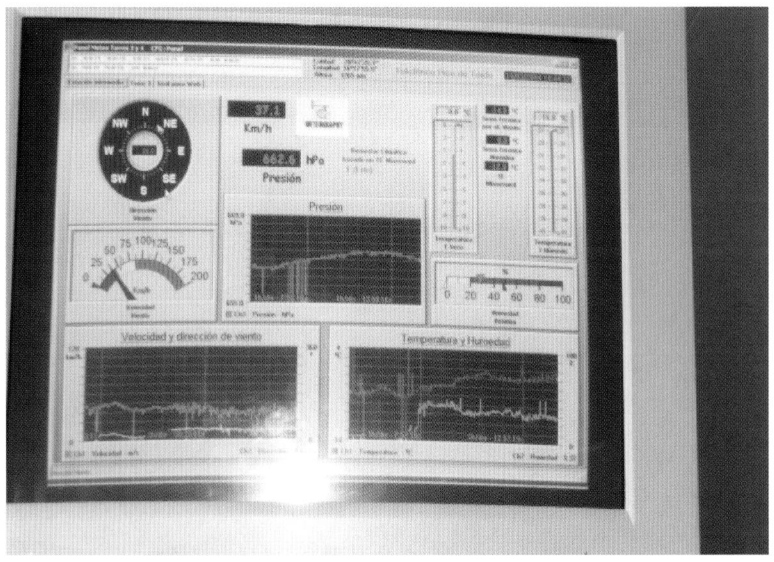

The Cable car station monitors the temperature, wind speed and direction.

Safety features include sensors on the pylons which constantly record the weather conditions; sometimes the temperature and wind are less at the top station than the bottom.

Mercado Fraga
An impressive variety of goods is sold in this shop.

A wise workman in Adeje

The finished Corpus Christi carpet

The end of a wonderful day

After a gathering in Santa Cruz of about 2000 retired musicians from around the island. Between me and my good friend Paca is our wonderful teacher, Mari Carmen.

At Easter, on Good Friday, La Pasión is broadcast live on television

La Pasión begins

La Pasión begins

glad of the opportunity to talk to Chris Francis, a pilot staying in the same accommodation. He'd come from the UK for the busy Falklands summer months when an extra pilot was needed to fly visitors and shearers from settlement to settlement.

One evening, as Chris drew planes on beer mats, he said, "Anyone can learn to fly a plane, if they have enough money."

I wondered if I could learn. The skills of the pilots here had impressed me because although the landing strips were short, they might frighten timid flyers, I heard of no accidents or fatalities. Flying here felt a lot safer than in Europe's increasingly overcrowded air spaces. Planes were the only transport communication for those living on the remote islands, they were a life line. Prior to landing, a competent local person was nearby. He was both fireman (behind his Land Rover he towed a fire extinguisher on a sledge) and an air traffic controller (he told the approaching pilot the wind speed and direction).

The last day of racing was replaced by steer-riding and this I was determined not to miss. Land Rovers, their windscreens glinting in the sun, were parked an impressive three deep around the huge square space where the action would take place. The bull made a swift entrance into the arena and after rapidly depositing a succession of brave men on the ground it was efficiently rounded up. Then one rider didn't move. With a broken hip he faced the long flight back to the UK for treatment. The hospital in Stanley catered for general health problems only. The people in the campo had a medical chest in their homes and early most mornings they could discuss their problems by radio with a doctor. One lady explained her illness and asked for medicine.

Immediately my host said, "She won't get those pills, she's had too many."

He was right. This time-slot was popular listening!

While in Stanley I had the back-breaking experience of helping Kevin, his wife Jan and Bridget, his mother, to 'rickle', turn over peat bricks so they were dried thoroughly by the sun and wind. Now I understood why some houses had converted to time-saving oil stoves. Both the wonderful smell of burning peat and the brightly painted wood houses *were* the Falklands. Unlike the UK's supermarket shelves that were full of varied fresh fruit and vegetables, here they were in short supply. The enterprising Hydroponics Company had built fibreglass cover wind-breaks and with the help of peat and oil heating fuel they grew much needed fresh tomatoes, lettuce and cucumber.

Some supplies came to the Falklands by boat, but this year it had broken down - with the turkeys for Christmas! If the store in Stanley had sold out of tin openers, you borrowed from a neighbour until supplies arrived. Many people had a vegetable plot, always protected from the wind by a square of tough gorse bushes, but even then only root vegetables, mostly potatoes, could thrive in the almost constant force 4 winds. Greenhouses were a rarity. A supply ship visited remote island settlements every three months.

I'd been looking forward to a New Year's Eve walk with my friend and this time he'd escaped from military responsibilities, work and social! It was wonderful to have the company of this special man who had unfailingly supported me during the worst time of my life. We hitchhiked to the isolated Great Britain Hotel, about half way along the road to Mount Pleasant, then walked to Fitzroy. The sun shone, a strong wind blew and the lonely Guards' monument reminded us of the horrors that had happened in this quiet, remote, beautiful spot. Here on Tuesday 8th June 1982, the *Sir Galahad* was mortally damaged, burned out and was later towed out to sea and sunk as a war gave. Although *Sir Tristram* was also badly damaged, she later returned to the UK to be repaired. At the end of this very special day, we parted at the roadside to hitch in opposite directions to all that the New Year might bring and to our futures.

Now it was time to visit Eileen Vidal, the exceptional lady who would help me to visit settlements during my last three weeks. She had the amazing capability of being able to talk on the radio to one person, to answer the phone and to talk to the person in front of her desk, all whilst writing down a message from an earlier call. She knew everyone and she arranged my visits to different islands by radioing people.

She said, "I have a lady here, she's from Wales, she's very nice, can you put her up for the nights of .....?"

When all had been confirmed, I went to the Falkland Island Government Air Service, FIGAS, and booked my flights.

The glamorous, photogenic, red Islander plane left Stanley airfield daily to land at as many settlements as possible within its fuel range. If sheep were wet, shearers couldn't work and their flight to the next settlement was delayed. Inevitably the plane's schedule was never the same on two days running. The names/destinations of those travelling were broadcast on the radio the evening before departure, guaranteeing that everyone knew everyone else's whereabouts! As with all aircraft, pilots calculate the plane's weight and balance prior to take off - so the 8-seater Islander's equipment list included a bathroom scale! Travelling with all my anti-allergenic bedding meant that I couldn't take as many bottles of whisky as I would have liked - gifts for my generous hosts - but I took as many as possible!

Situated at sea level on Falkland Sound, the straits that separate East and West Falkland, was Port Howard Lodge. This atmospheric, original building with its genuine, creaky floorboards was a popular base for fishermen. Robin Lee, the delightfully positive owner, accepted that a lone *fe*male wanted to explore and was wonderfully encouraging and helpful. Soon after arrival I set off to walk up Mount Maria, 2158ft (660m). Robin's only advice was to avoid the well-marked mined areas on the lower slopes and if in trouble to light a fire. However this should be a very last resort because, if fire got established in the peat, it would be difficult, if not impossible, to put out.

Without paths, walking through dried-up, inedible Diddle-dee berries was hard going and the power of the sun was strong enough to burn me slightly, even though my shirt was off for a very short time. I'd forgotten about the conflict as I approached the summit when suddenly the detritus of war, camouflage netting, shovels and jerry cans, was all around. I wanted to stay here for a while to absorb the atmosphere and just think my thoughts but it seemed wisest not to delay for too long. Going downhill on rough ground with a torn cartilage and loose knee ligaments needed care.

I was delighted when the next day Robin took me to visit his young sons who were camping on a beach miles from home, learning real self-reliance in this safe environment. From the air I'd seen an isolated river of stones that stood out in sharp contrast with only ground-hugging vegetation all around them.

As his Land Rover bumped over a 'run' of stones Robin said, "There are many theories about the stones but they have no obvious source."

Then we left a track and went across country to a tiny bay where the boys had a fire on the only safe place, the pebbly beach. Upland Geese were easy to catch because when chased they soon ran out of puff; their legs were on the grill - and cans of Coca-Cola were hidden beneath the flysheet! Leaving them in peace Robin took me to Rosalea Cottage. If I could return here with friends - as I wished - there were first ascents of nearby 2,000ft (600m) unclimbed hills waiting to be plucked - for the Alpine Club records? Only the nearby gallows frame looked out of place, until he explained that from it would hang our meat supply. This wonderful man even put his boat on the water so that I could have the fun of watching the dolphins playing 'last to cross in front of the bow'. I joined the many who failed to photograph anything more than a splash, but being so near to these magnificent creatures was enough.

I'd been pleased that here, unlike the UK, no animal was indoors. It was my hostess, Biffo, on Saunders Island who explained why Falkland Islanders' dogs lived outside. In the countryside there was Hydatid, a microscopic tapeworm found in foxes, dogs and cats. Cases of Hydatid in humans were rare but when they did occur they caused parasitic tumours. She also said that I should visit the nesting ground of a spectacular and very large colony of Black Browed Albatross. Its dramatic position was well worth the four-hour walk because huge adult birds were using the updrafts and gliding near the cliff edge. In the foreground their nests, solid pillars of mud touched up with seaweed and grass, were re-used annually and a proud, photogenic chick posed for my perfect picture.

Sea Lion Island was about a mile (1.6kms) wide and 4 miles (6.5kms) long and in its purpose-built lodge there was a bar with background music and videos of killer whales to see. The atmosphere resembled a first-class hotel and the conversation varied between pilots comparing the dangers of flying Chinook helicopters with other types of helicopters, to priest, Father John, chatting about South Georgia. He even offered to help me to go there by boat but sadly the time needed was greater than I wanted to be away from my mother.

Meanwhile I sat for hours, fascinated, watching male elephant seals, weighing up to four tons, suddenly rise up and clout each other for no apparent reason. Overseeing this unprovoked aggression, from the safety of her nest above the beach, was a grand old female Striated Caracara, known locally as Johnny Rook. She had a very attentive young husband! This large bird of prey is a powerful predator, ridiculously tame, vulnerable to persecution and one of the rarest birds in the world. But perhaps the most spectacular scene was the Rockhopper penguins' perseverance and skill in battling with the huge waves crashing against a cliff. Their route was up a rock slab whose steep, diagonal slope hugged the wall as it ascended to where I sat. Time after time, waves sucked penguin after penguin back into the sea. I was impressed. It was a lesson in determination.

My last night in the campo at Port Louis, a mere 'pop' from Stanley, was with splendid hosts, Mike and Sue Morrison. Their garden was full of vegetables and it brought home to me yet again that the benefits of peaceful countryside living were paid for by non-stop, back-breaking hard physical work. In 1981, before the conflict, the number of people living in the campo was approximately equal to that in Stanley, but by 1986 that number was half of that in Stanley. The 2006 census gave non-military resident numbers as 2955 in Stanley and 363 in the campo. As I was leaving the Falklands, Kevin Donnelly and others were investigating the possibility of regular supplies and flights from South America. These are now running and the Hydroponics Company supplies visiting cruise ships with some fresh items.

The hospitality that I received everywhere was unstinting; the time had sped by, the flight home was trouble free but the excitement had not ended. A lot of patchy ground fog was all around as the heavily loaded Tristar was coming in to land. The whole plane fell silent and very still when, at the last moment, full power was applied and after what seemed an eternity it began to take effect. Gradually the loaded plane hauled itself back into the air, went around and next time landed perfectly.

Chapter 11
Airborne

I hoped that my interesting photos and maps of the Falklands might help to divert my mother from her limitations. While her strength was gradually ebbing away she remained, as always, a courageous, good listener and her mind was as sharp as ever.

Carelessly I said, "I got a book off Ann."

Her immediate reply was, "From, from, from, you can't get a book off anyone!"

It was torture to see her in this state and I found visits increasingly difficult.

Again I was in need of something else to divert my worries and Chris's words were ringing in my head, "Anyone can learn to fly, if they have the money". With considerable trepidation, on 8th February 1989, I went to Caernarfon Airport for a trial flight. It was my fiftieth year and this would be my present to myself.

It was a month after I had returned from the Falkland Islands and when I saw the tiny, low-wing, single-engine Cherokee 140 I was overawed by the thought of flying it. While my instructor, Peter, introduced me to the various parts of the plane, I got only a general impression, understood little and remembered even less. The plane was tiny and the language was awesome.

When we had gained height I had to stop being an overwhelmed, passive observer.

Peter said, "You take control."

I hadn't expected the plane's response to be so sensitive or that such intense concentration would be needed just to keep flying straight and level. While aiming for a cloud, or distant hill, I mustn't rivet my gaze on a feature. Regularly I had to scan three important instruments: the direction indicator (DI) the altimeter and the air speed indicator (ASI) while maintaining an accurate heading and altitude. It all seemed very logical.

One trial flight led to another until I bought the first of five excellent Trevor Thom flying training manuals. I was hooked. My lump sum that I should save for old age would be my fiftieth birthday present - to me. This intimidating new environment brought, like the army, its own language and another ladder to climb. Turning the control wheel to the left moved the ailerons that were on the trailing edge of the wing, farthest from the cabin. This turned the plane to the left. During a 360° turn I had to hold the control wheel steady all the while maintaining the same height. So I tried to keep one spot on the cowling moving along the horizon, between sky and land or sea, as if painting a straight line - while not forgetting to scan the dials! I knew I'd been successful if, at the end of the 360° turn, we were buffeted by our shockwaves.

Gradually, my repertoire of skills increased. Straight climbs and descents led to climbing and descending turns, all the while scanning the instruments. But when using the radio, words in my head wouldn't come out of my mouth. And the phonetic Alpha Beta alphabet didn't help. The plane's call sign, GAYIG, was Golf Alpha Yankee India Golf - or Golf-India Golf for short. All the time Peter impressed upon me that if the nose was too high, air speed would start to drop and if this continued it would result in the plane spinning downwards. Should this happen near to landing there would be insufficient height and time to correct the spin and the plane would crash!

Small planes often have only one door and many rarely fly much above 3,000ft, too low for a parachute to open, so they didn't carry them. For emergencies the syllabus included practice forced landings (PFLs). With the engine power at idle, but warmed at regular intervals, I had to look for that miracle – a flat field that was 'into wind' and minus telephone wires, animals or oil seed rape! Pilots who regularly practised PFLs had the best chance of walking away from the plane. Instructor, Nigel Baston, did just that. Flying from Mona airfield,

Anglesey, at night, he had engine failure when on base leg. The strong easterly wind prevented them from reaching the runway but on touch down it stopped the plane inches before a hedge. Although the plane was damaged, the three occupants exited unscathed!

I didn't envy instructors the nail-biting task of sitting next to the student who was learning to take off and to land, called 'doing circuits' or 'touch and go'. Moving the flaps, situated on the trailing edge of the wing nearest to the cabin, affects the position of the nose of the plane and therefore the pilot's view of the runway. Full flap brought a lower approach speed and the plane's nose pointed steeply downwards, an aid when landing on tiny airstrips. The view was excitingly similar to a descent on the Big Dipper!

Like many students I hit a learning 'block' while trying to land - even when the wind was at its kindest, blowing straight down the runway! In the Falklands I'd seen Chris landing using the 'crab' method with the nose pointing sideways, into a cross wind, until the point of touch down. But my ruthlessly logical mind kept wondering how any beginner, older than the bright seventeen-year old who goes solo after 5-7 hours' training, ever learned this split-second timing.

Eventually the day came for my first solo flight. I knew that I was ready but I wondered if it would be possible because the dismal, grey sky and land blended into one. The usual clear horizon was missing. At the end of our first warm-up circuit we were near to touch down when we hit a seagull.

"Stop the plane," was Peter's immediate response.

We taxied to a halt near the refuelling area where we washed off a surprising amount of blood that splattered the plane's white wings and hooked bits of gut from behind the propeller. Although one end of Caernarfon airport's runway was metres from the sea and gulls were all around, bird strikes were rare, possibly one a year. But it was even more unusual to have this happen on the circuit prior to going solo!

As we completed another circuit Peter said, "Stop the plane."

He got out, my heart rate shot up – this was it! I realised why a medical was required before going solo. At the end of the runway, with my heart thumping, I completed the checks, took off but I hadn't expected that without the instructor's weight the little plane tipped slightly to my side. When the downwind radio and other checks were

Flying in Florida
Solo downwind to land at Naples Airport.

Finals to land at Mona Airfield, Anglesey
When approaching to land on runway 04 pilots should be above 200 ft when they pass over the A5 Holyhead Road. It is very near to this end of the runway.

done, and the turns onto base leg and finals completed, the runway was approaching, fast, and suddenly it was all over. Early in my training, after only 30 minutes' flying I'd used up my reserves of concentration but gradually my flying time increased. However, on the day I went solo it was a relief to be safely and reasonably competently back on the ground. It was all over in 10 minutes. I was left on an adrenaline high, drained of energy. Having reached my half-century, my fourteen hours training did not seem too disgraceful.

From then on solo circuits alternated with navigation training plus a few hours of flying non-visual with the ground. This was to convince learners that they would need another course before they could fly solo into cloud, at night or even when an anticyclone reduced visibility by compressing pollution and pollen to ground level. After studying the map for what felt like only a few seconds, on checking the instruments the plane could be flying off course, height or both. Radio work was another necessary distraction from checking the dials. When concentrating on a map it was easy to miss a call from an air traffic controller - and they don't like to say things twice!

Peter's constant reminder was, "Fly the plane first, everything else comes afterwards."

My next challenge was the complex procedures required to approach airports. Meticulous preparation and planning for cross-country flights, including an up-to-date weather forecast for wind direction and speed, was vital; these factors affected the time of arrival at all the points en route. Changes of radio frequencies, airfields' different landing procedures and other factors also had to be researched because all planes entering an airport's airspace were positioned by the air traffic controllers; pilots who entered this controlled area without their permission could receive impressive fines! But surprises still lay ahead.

On my first flight to Liverpool Airport with an instructor the air traffic controller said, "Orbit at the mushroom."

But this local landmark was not on the aeronautical chart. It was a wonderfully exciting experience to be landing here again on my solo cross-country test while hearing radio calls from incoming commercial pilots.

As I touched down, the controller said, "Expedite!"

I taxied fast to the exit.

The minimum time to qualify for the Private Pilot Licence was 45 hours but weather, lesson frequency, the pilot's age and ability and not least the instructor could affect the hours required. Luckily I met only one instructor who made concentration difficult by filling my headset with his grumbles! On the 3rd July 1989 I passed the final exam with a paltry 10 hours and 55 minutes solo flights but a whopping 57 hours dual - due to some non-syllabus, long, cross-country flights!

When my logbook had been authorised and returned by the Civil Aviation Authority, CAA, I'd moved to Mona Flying Club on Anglesey, where on weekdays we were grounded because the RAF Hawk pilots practised landings. Now the proud owner of a Private Pilot's Licence, PPL, I could take a passenger in the two-seater, single-engine Cessna. Maggie Adam was my first, brave passenger. During my years of commuting between Folkestone and Bangor, this faithful friend had remembered when I'd be home and she always rang to tell me the local news. Before take-off I'd given her all the briefings; however, approaching to land in the small plane was slower than she had expected. Only as we taxied, did she admit that she'd nearly run out of the breath she was holding until touch down.

After some consideration, I decided to tell my mother what I was doing.

I said, "You know I've done crazy things like climbing and I expect you'll think I'm mad but I'm learning to fly."

What a brave mother she was; she'd always said that her worst nightmare was me dying before her.

But after a pause she smiled and, always encouraging, said, "No, I'm very proud of you."

Once I was qualified, like driving a car, I knew that time and experience were needed to apply my skills in a wide variety of conditions. But that autumn I was grounded by the UK winter weather, the availability of the plane or my mother's needs. My fragile competence was at risk of being lost when I was told about low-cost flying in America. On 23rd January 1990, exactly a year after I had returned from the Falklands, I was on a Pan Am flight to Miami.

I'd never been to America before and I was impressed by how genuinely kind everyone was. I passed quickly through immigration - after I'd said that I had a pilot's licence and was coming for three weeks to gain experience! I found the instructor waiting for me in another part of the airport and, although tired, I flew a different type of plane, a Piper Tomahawk, the 90-minute flight from Miami to Naples airfield on the West Coast of Florida.

Next day, after an hour of ground school to familiarise me with local flying conditions, an instructor took me to the car rental office and left me there. Luckily the kind lady in the office gave me a map of Naples and had time to point out the route to my accommodation. With the high temperatures and humidity the car's powerful air conditioning was bliss - once I'd been shown how to work it and the automatic gears! It was a relief to be back in my accommodation.

I'd been unwilling to break the journey from the UK with a night in Miami so now I had to return there to register my PPL licence with the Federal Aviation Authority, FAA. The exciting experience of approaching Miami airport with an instructor in a tiny, low powered plane was well worth the cost of the return flight. It was the fastest final descent to land that I'd flown; we were embedded in a long line of large commercial planes that couldn't reduce their speed any further.

Back in Naples each checkout, the cross-country, circuits and the unusual attitudes (steep turns and stalls) was done with a different instructor but none would sign me off to fly alone. On top of this, the accommodation was poor, the fridge was dirty and I was desperate. It takes a lot to break me but when I went to Naples Air Centre, the other flying school on the airfield, I was near to tears and ready to give up flying. Every day was precious, I doubted that I'd ever return to Florida and the first week out of three had gone. John Whittle, the boss, could not have been kinder.

He took me to his office saying, "You're not the first and you won't be the last to come from that school."

John also offered me accommodation to rent at Bonita Springs, a 30 minute drive from Naples. 'Residents' on the Imperial River Court Mobile Home Park were regular winter 'snow birds' and for the next two weeks I enjoyed their good company. Being a solo traveller it was wonderful to be able to share my experiences with others. Best of all was that wisely I'd not paid three weeks' money 'up front' to the other mob.

In the UK I'd not flown a high-wing Cessna plane before, nor had I mastered cross-wind landings and with many single runways in

Florida these skills were urgently needed. Luckily instructor Carl Boot taught me another method, the wing down into the prevailing cross wind. By putting my hands and feet lightly on the control column and rudder pedals I could feel what he was doing and I 'got it' right away. With 12 days left all that I had dreamed about came true. I flew with a flask in my bag and a towel under my bottom. With high humidity outside the cockpit and much concentration-generated sweat inside I needed protection from the plastic seats!

Now I saw why the USA was called the Big Country. The roads were wide, supermarket aisles were not cramped collision routes for overloaded trolleys and Naples town felt decadent with personal space around the houses. American English was different.

On one long flight my radio call was, "Routing to Williston", a phrase in common use, if not standard procedure.

There was silence before the controller said, "Where'd you say you're going Ma'am?"

Recruiting student pilots at RAF Valley Air Show

I flew this Cessna from Mona airfield to RAF Valley only 8 miles away.

I answered with even greater care.

This time the silence was broken by another pilot, "I think the lady said routing to Williston!"

My speech was relatively free from any UK difficult-to-understand regional accent.

When solo, at first I returned to airfields that I'd visited with instructors. There was always free help-yourself percolator coffee and often it was a person serving in a shop who answered my radio call. Owning a plane was regarded much as owning a second car was in the UK. With plenty of uncontrolled air space, away from airports, I needed constantly to scan the horizon. It was important to avoid close encounters with a similar kind because here it was not uncommon for small planes to fly without radios. Also two airfields with the same runway direction could be within radio range. Runway 17-35 refers to the direction of the compass. On approach to an airfield and when landing, as well as keeping an eagle eye out for non-radioed planes, I radioed, "Downwind for runway 35 at *Marco Island*", followed by, "Finals for runway 35 at *Marco Island*".

It was bliss to have America's excellent, free, weather forecasts for pilots that was light years ahead of anything available at that time in the UK; I could speak directly to the met man. He not only routed me around storm clouds but also told me about important additional pilot-reported weather problems, such as wind sheer, which can make landings difficult and dangerous. Gradually I flew further and for longer. I wanted to get as much experience as possible and I never passed an airfield without landing.

My first real, self-inflicted fright was about forty minutes' flying time south of Naples at the Everglades. This short airstrip had water at both ends and trees beside the runway, which could cause wind sheer. I was on the final approach to land when suddenly I was eye to eye with a pelican. My avoiding swerve was completed just before I began the struggle to land the plane that was severely affected by downdrafts. It took longer than expected before the wheels finally touched terra firma; immediately, but gently, I pushed the throttle forward to full power; this mustn't be done too quickly. I was airborne just before the runway ended.

Before I left Naples to fly to Key West International I had to file a flight plan giving the details of the plane, the occupants and my times of departure and landing. Should I have an engine failure there was little dry land en route. I activated the plan on take off and it had to be cancelled within a short time of touch down or emergency procedures would have gone into action. In perfect weather I planned to fly south along the edge of the Everglades with their alligators and then turn 90° along the Keys.

On Sundays the skies were busy and as I approached the Keys I was keeping a good lookout for planes when the comms dial for radio frequencies went blank. Putting maps around the windscreen to shield them from the sun didn't help and I was frightened. The air traffic controller was too busy to talk to me, he just kept telling me to change frequency. Then suddenly I sensed that something was wrong. The air speed indicator was in the red, well above cruising speed. Distracted by the comms problem, I was heading towards the sea, fast.

I remembered Peter's frequent reminder to, 'Fly the plane first' and when back in 'straight and level' I orbited to give myself time to think. I'd 'lost' my frequency. I couldn't go to Key West and I needed to talk to someone so I climbed to 5,000ft where I hoped to have better radio range. I did. My first request to the sympathetic controller who answered was *not* to be told to change frequency and the second was to close my flight plan. He listened to my problem and couldn't have been more helpful. With his frequency I could count the changes needed to contact Naples and there would be no 'British lady pilot in trouble' headlines in newspapers. He called me at regular intervals to check that all was well as I retraced my route and his friendly support was much appreciated.

At Naples an instructor showed me another ring on the comms dial that was smaller than a fingernail. I had flown this plane for only a few hours, none of them at night when a dazzled pilot might use this dimmer switch. I was relieved to be told that on a steep turn it can and had 'dropped off'. I put it all down to experience, refuelled and immediately popped over to Marco Island for another landing. Here the airport directory said, 'and risk of alligators crossing the runway.' As I approached the threshold, their snouts were visible, poking out of the water. It had been a memorable day.

However, the highlight of my time in Florida was a visit to Gwen and Alan Gardner. They had sold their caravan park in Bethesda, North

Wales, to move to Indian River near Vero Beach on Florida's East Coast. En route I landed at Pahokee by huge Okeechobee Lake in the centre of Florida, a perfect spot for a rest and a coffee. It was an idyllic setting and I still found it hard to believe that I was here, having the skies for my playground and a convenient railway line to help navigation to the Garners. On the ground, Alan used his hand held radio to tell me the wind speed and direction before I did my first landing on grass, where the wheels wouldn't run as freely as they do on tarmac. Concentrating every second I was thankful to land safely, not to disgrace myself and to enjoy Gwen's excellent lunch.

The holiday was a thrilling experience and gradually my three hours' flying a day increased to four, then five and six. To make the most of my last day I flew 7.3 hours, making my total hours flying solo in America to about forty and I looked forward to telling my mother about this very special holiday.

Although I knew that she wouldn't recover, it was still a shock when my mother died two months later, on 31st March 1990. I found it hard to believe that I'd lost the support of the one person who had never, ever, let me down and I've never ceased to miss her supportive congratulations, commiserations and encouragement.

Two days before her death, just as I was leaving she said, "I'm sick of all this".

Although I knew that for her it was a release from the indignities of having to be fed and 'topped and tailed' by strangers, I couldn't believe that she was gone.

Thanks to keeping in contact with Ron and Ginny, we visit when nearby, when they rented an apartment in Calpe, Costa Blanca, they invited me, and other friends to stay. The timing couldn't have been better. It was wonderful to be back on warm rock where muscles began to remember old habits; by now Ron had added mountain biking to his sporting activities, climbing and golf. Had I not been there with them in a bar in Calpe I would never have heard about Tenerife.

Chapter 12
El Teide magic

In the company of Ron and Ginny, I was having my first encounter with karaoke's aural assault in a bar in Calpe when a tall, handsome stranger walked in. With high, protruding cheekbones and unusually deep hollows beneath, I could neither keep my eyes off him, nor decide whether he was well tanned or had naturally dark skin. When he stood near me I couldn't resist taking the opportunity to speak to him.

"Why don't you sing?" I asked.

"I'm a professional singer so I can't," was his prompt reply. "My job is to attract visitors into the bar."

He was looking forward to leaving in three days' time to work in Tenerife, so I was surprised and pleased when he returned the next evening. We were playing pool; he joined us and I heard more about his plans. A week later I mentioned this encounter to a friend in Bangor, Pam Marchant.

"I'm going to Tenerife in two weeks' time, you can come with me if you want but we'll have to find you somewhere to stay," was her response.

Warm weather sounded very attractive because I was on crutches having had the inside of my knee scraped. On a map I found Tenerife, near the bulge of Africa, about 2000 miles from the UK and I looked forward to visiting another remote island. I was in for a shock.

In January 1992, our delayed flight landed at Tenerife South Airport at 2200hrs and every baggage carousel was surrounded by British voices. Friday was the timeshare owners' changeover day. Pam's friend, John, was renovating her very basic cottage in the hills and he met us at the airport. Soon we discovered that all the hotel accommodation in Los Cristianos was booked and it was midnight before we found a pension, but sleep was impossible because the bedroom walls allowed all inmates to hear every sound.

With a disturbed night came the inevitable scratching and next morning I discovered that my Ventolin asthma inhaler did not work. Added to finding better accommodation I wanted a chemist, but breakfast was my first priority. Once I had confirmed that Ventolin was available and my lungs were not unhappy, I postponed buying it and began my search for decent accommodation.

In the plaza facing the church in Los Cristianos was a small estate agent's office. Here a miracle happened.

Although the man behind the desk had apartments to rent, generously he said to a person nearby, "Bill, you have a place to rent don't you?"

After I'd seen and declined the agent's ground floor apartments, Bill Foster took me to see his studio on the second floor in the superbly designed complex, Pueblo Torviscas, situated near the end of Playa de Las Américas. Unlike the other apartments that I'd seen, here you'd have to be Houdini to get from one balcony to another, vertically or horizontally. At night only one entrance to the complex remained open; a security guard patrolled and here I felt safe.

Lying beside a pool all day was not for me. I travelled to explore places and my challenge now was where to go in the daytime and, more difficult, the evenings. Luckily, from package holidays with Ron I knew that holiday representatives' information books were left in the foyer of big hotels. In the Esmeralda hotel across the road I read about TITSA, the bus company whose green buses I'd seen hopping off in all directions like crickets in summer. At 0915hrs a bus, 342, departed to El Teide National Park. What could be better? But next day, at 0915hrs, I was frustrated because 'the bus never arrived' – a complaint that I would hear frequently in the future! I had joined the many first time visitors, and even some locals, who had misunderstood the bus timetable. Once a day it left the Las Américas bus station, some bus stops further on, at 0915hrs!

My crutches on the col, approximately half way up Guajara

Once we'd left the coast behind and were steadily gaining height, we were surrounded by a dry, barren, cactus-covered landscape scattered with low-level cottages and small communities. Then, quite suddenly, the scenery changed to carefully-tended terraced fields of potatoes with vines around the edges and a long, straight stretch of road brought us to the attractive village, Vilaflor, nestling into a horseshoe of hillside.

At about 5,000ft (1524m) it was the highest village in Tenerife - and in Spain! From here we were surrounded by pines and could catch only occasional glimpses of the coastline until, to my surprise and the delight of all the passengers, the driver stopped in a lay-by. He indicated that we could get out because here there was a perfect view of the islands of La Gomera and La Palma. We appreciated the opportunity of this 10-minute photo stop because there was no rush; the bus would begin its return journey at 1515hrs.

We were above the tree line when a sharp right-hand bend brought an abrupt change of scenery. We were surrounded by dramatic lava flows, their colours varying from black to red, yellow to near white, all frozen in time. We'd arrived at the Cañadas - flat sandy areas - and it was easy to visualise the fiery hot cinders tumbling over each other in their relentless progress over near horizontal ground. The landscape was awesome. Above the road at about 7,000ft (2134m) jagged-edged volcanic peaks circled around us.

Curious to see where the journey ended, I stayed on the bus. After a 10-minute 'comfort' stop at the splendid Parador del Teide, a hotel and restaurant, we went a mere four kilometres before the remaining passengers were dropped off by the cable car. From here it was an 8-minute ascent to the top station, 162m (531ft) below the summit of El Teide – at 12,198ft (3718m) the highest mountain in the Canary Islands and in Spain!

For the remainder of the journey my eyes darted between the stunning scenery and watching the driver's skill when negotiating the many bends on this barely two-coach wide road. At El Portillo he parked and, speaking only Spanish, he pointed to a notice in the bus reminding passengers that it departed at 1515hrs. I didn't know that there was a Visitors' Centre at the lower El Portillo over a kilometre further downhill to the north. To sit in one of the three bars for four hours was impossible and exploring on rough ground was unwise. I tried sign language to the driver and he seemed to understand that I'd crutch the 11 kilometres back to the cable car.

It was hard on my under-arms, but frequent rests gave me time to see at close quarters and to touch the different rock textures. Pumice, light in weight and colour, contrasted with the nearby black, shiny, sharp obsidian that had been evacuated from El Teide's womb. The driver seemed to be a kind man but, despite my confidence that he wouldn't leave me behind, when the friendly green bus appeared in sight my heart leapt. My affection for the TITSA buses had begun.

The sparkling, rugged beauty of the Cañadas was unlike anywhere I'd been before. I had to return. My guidebook [1] described an 'easy walk on pahoe lava' to some caves so a few days later I was back, crutching my way alongside the García rocks opposite the Parador. The easy, wide path soon narrowed and, while stopping for rests, my eyes were drawn away from the rocks to the cable cars passing each other as they gently

---

[1] *Landscapes of Southern Tenerife and La Gomera* by Noel Rochford. Sunflower books, 1988

ascended and descended. The temperature was perfect, the sun shone and the purity of the air gave my lungs an ecstasy-like energy.

Although surrounded by crumbling, unpleasant to walk on red volcanic rubble, the grey A-shaped area of the pahoe lava stood out clearly and at its centre, where I guessed that the caves should be, I spotted a group. Hoping that they would not move, I headed towards them as fast as the rubber bungs on my crutches allowed. The guidebook was right: this pahoe lava had grip-fix adhesive power. And there beside a cave were four members of the London Philharmonic Orchestra. They were relaxing between concerts in Santa Cruz in the north, the island capital. It was good to have their company and we had time to chat over coffee at the Parador before both our buses departed at 1600hrs, theirs to Puerto de la Cruz and mine to Las Américas.

Before returning home I couldn't resist a third visit to the stunning scenery of the Cañadas. Emerging from the 342 bus, this time the air temperature was decidedly cooler but, thanks to the power of the sun,

Garcia rocks and the Parador, viewed from the summit of Guajara

both my sweater and jacket remained in my rucksack as I crutched my way along a wide, easy, very dusty track behind the Parador. My goal was Guajara 2718m (8917ft) high. The guide book's accuracy impressed me. The very discreet pile of stones marking the start of the real ascent was there.

Now the tiny path winding its way uphill between bushes wasn't obvious but my goal, the skyline, was. I was amazed to meet no hill walkers. The solitude, the peace and the beauty of the scenery was all a mountaineer could want. Then suddenly the path went into shade. With crutches strategically placed, carefully I negotiated the ice and soon I was on the ridge in sunshine. From here the Parador looked like a doll's house and the cars resembled dinky toys. However, mountain rescues had taught me that most accidents occur during *descents*. The walk had taken me longer than I'd expected, so after a rest and a photograph of my crutches propped up on a rock to prove I'd been there, I descended, carefully. The summit could wait for my next visit!

Stunning scenery, lungs freed from inhalers, and the 342 driver's kindness and reliability had given me perfect days out. Three times I'd left the Cañadas in brilliant sunshine, but before we'd reached Vilaflor we'd descended into thick cloud. On my first visit I thought that I was in luck - but three times? I discovered that it was not unusual for a layer of cloud, about 305m (1,000ft) thick, to gather around midday, its position depending upon the air pressure. Indeed, it was a common and regular occurrence. In winter, from December to March, sunbathers at the coast would look up, see the cloud and not realise that above it conditions were perfect. But when the forecast for the whole island was grim, rain falls at the coast and snow, along with high winds at altitude, would close the road.

Solo travellers loaded with cases found relief with the arrival of spacious handicapped toilets, but at first I found no comfort stops for evenings. To hide away in Bill's studio was not what life was about and to dine in a restaurant required the defence of a book - but even this could not be drawn out for long! What could I do to solve this problem? In Las Américas, an area furiously touristic, browsing in shops seemed to be the only activity other than eating and drinking.

As soon as I sat down at a bar I was pounced upon by a waiter's, "What will you have to drink?"

And the eagle eye of the manager ensured the waiter's hovering began as soon as my glass was empty, if not before. So I ate in the apartment rather than face the waiter looking behind my shoulder for the appearance of a partner, prior to conducting me to a table. However, by 2100hrs musical 'entertainment' - of a volume intolerable for my ears - had started in bars. They were in direct line-of-sound to my balcony doors. From then until midnight the singer's voice was so loud that I kept reading the same sentence over and over again. I was forced to go out.

Although it was a needle-in-a-haystack hope, to give a purpose to the evening, and applying again the principle that you are not alone when you are travelling, I went to search for the handsome stranger. A linear return walk on crutches could extend either as far as my underarm strength allowed or to the proximity of a bus stop to catch the last bus back to Torviscas. Once the music had started in bars the drinks cost more so, with one exception, my 'research' was done from the pavement.

There were many bars with musicians, but I kept returning to Liverpudlian Graham Gold singing his country and western Johnny Cash songs on the terrace of the Banana Garden that was situated below the busy main road through Las Américas. (Several years later I did find the handsome stranger; he remembered me and he gave me a tape recording of his songs.) Graham was fun to watch, good to listen to and you never knew what he would do next. I saw no other singer with a radio mike, which freed him from a wall socket. While playing his guitar, Graham would sit on the knee of an attractive wife or bend down in front of a small child who watched him in wonder from a pram. The visitors loved it. His playing stopped as he climbed the wall, resumed on the pavement and even continued when, traffic allowing, he strayed onto the road. All this had the added bonus of attracting more clients to sit at the tables. When Graham's daughter videoed his performance, we could buy the video of him, his songs and us to take home. I did.

Graham and his wife, Leslie, played until 2300hrs, when she was replaced by Bright Englebert, a super bass player who had written the attractive song, 'Give it hope, Joanna', the name of his daughter. Whilst always enjoyable when these two experienced musicians played, some nights really 'took off' and a magical hour came to an end at midnight when outdoor music had to stop. 'Cinderella' returned to Bill's studio along a dark, deserted Hydrangea Walk, looking at the sea, which on some nights was lit by halogen strength moonlight. It reminded me of a night when I was a student in Bangor; we had gone up Snowdon in September by the light of a harvest moon. No head torches were needed.

Strolling around Las Américas every night was impossible; I was incapable of measuring my pleasure by the pint and there was a limit on how many unwanted orange juices I could drink. Twiglets of interesting conversation were in inverse proportion to the strength of trouser belt straining to support an avalanche of flesh. Las Américas seemed to be full of flocks of young singles hell bent on a drunken night out, older couples recycling pub chat and families. I could fill daytimes but I felt like a 'fish out of water' in the evenings until, by the entrance to Pueblo Torviscas, I found Stephan's unique, tiny bar. He was from mainland Spain, but his clients were British. Watching him in action, I was impressed at his ability to convince returning visitors, who always expected to be recognised, that he remembered them. Whenever he had time he talked to his customers, a lifeline for single travellers like me and for a surprising number of couples! When he heard that Bob Reaside, now retired from the engine room of a cross channel ferry, had a Private Pilot's Licence, we were introduced. It was good to meet someone with similar interests and eventually I summoned up the courage to ask Bob if he'd always been single.

Indignantly he answered, "No, I lived with my mother until I was 40!"

We have kept in contact ever since.

When Pam and John took me on a grand circuit of the island in their little blue van I realised how large Tenerife was, a total area of about 790sq miles (2046 square km). We were the only visitors enjoying a beer, fresh bread and local goat's cheese in perfect tranquillity at the attractive village of Masca, perched precariously on the crest of a steep-sided ridge. At Icod de Los Vinos we admired the famous Dragon Tree, the oldest and largest example in the world of the Dracaena Drago. A

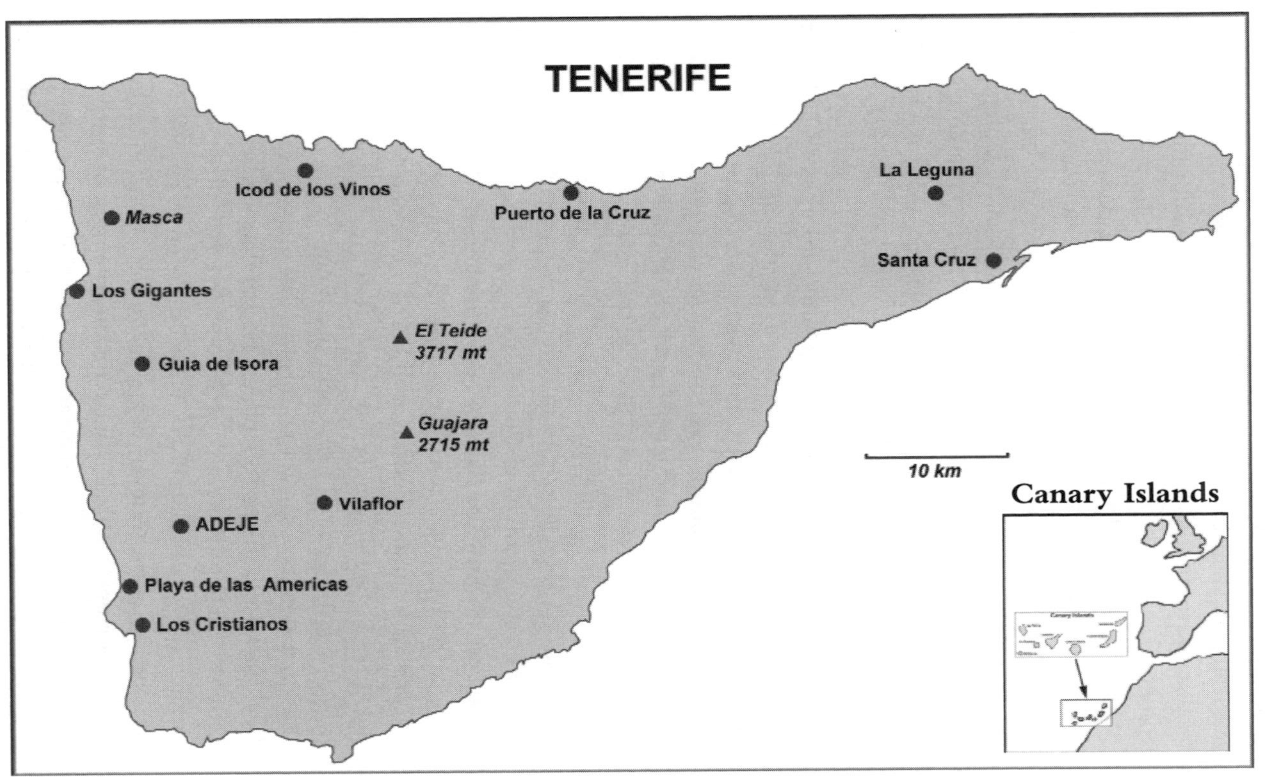
TENERIFE
Icod de los Vinos
Masca
Puerto de la Cruz
La Leguna
Santa Cruz
Los Gigantes
El Teide
3717 mt
Guia de Isora
Guajara
2715 mt
10 km
Canary Islands
Vilaflor
ADEJE
Playa de las Americas
Los Cristianos

Tenerife

native to these islands, this tree had a thousand branches, one for every year of its life. It was already 73 years old when William the Conqueror invaded England and, because its sap was famous for turning red when in contact with air, the tree's 'blood' had a reputation for medicinal purposes.

However, Pam and John were busy working on her cottage so I tried the 'free' buses to the banana garden plantation. We paid to enter and after the informative guided tour, done in several languages, we tasted their free thimble-sized glass of smooth banana liqueur; many visitors were tempted to buy some. At the Cactus Park, without a guide but with information leaflets in several languages, we were left to follow signs at leisure; a flattened, spiky round catcus called Mother-in-law's seat was unforgettable!

It had been a holiday fascinatingly different from any I'd had before and, thrilled that I'd not needed to use an inhaler until 24 hours after landing in Manchester, I had returned twice more that year. The inhaler stayed in my suitcase and it was good to be remembered by Nacho, Manolo and other staff in Pueblo Torviscas – and by Stephan!

In January, while the almond blossom was creating the wow-factor at lower altitudes, the temperature at the Cañadas in winter could vary from sun, strong enough to burn uncovered skin in a remarkably short time, to a vicious arctic wind. Sometimes, even when wearing my ski over-trousers, only my side that was facing the sun was warm - so I kept turning as though on a spit! There could be freezing cold, cloudy conditions with snow underfoot at El Portillo where cloud spills over the lip of the Cañadas from the north, while at the Parador only about 10 miles away, it was snow-free, warm and sunny.

In severe conditions it was no surprise that snow blocked the road to the Cañadas and stopped all traffic. The island needed the snow that soaked into the porous volcanic rock and filled the galleries inside the mountain; heavy rainfall at lower altitudes tended to run off into the sea. But predominant were my happy memories of sitting on the steps of the Parador after a walk in winter, making the most of every minute in the dramatic scenery and pure air while waiting for Arcadio and his 342 bus. Below Vilaflor not only did we emerge from cloud, we descended into another world!

By April snowfalls were rare, the first plants began to blossom and by May and June the Cañadas wore its coat of many colours. Bees were busy collecting the purest honey that could be bought. The ugly, upward pointing rats-tail-like stems of Ratama del Teide had been transformed to a scent-laden large football of pink/white flowers and Cordeso's fuzzy stems had a beautiful yellow coat. But all too soon the high summer temperatures made the Cañadas a witch's cauldron of heat, the floral display faded rapidly and the rock climbers from Santa Cruz migrated to northern Europe.

I had both experienced and observed the difficulty foreigners had when travelling on the buses so, with doubt about the outcome, I offered an article, 'Ticket to Ride', about the buses, to the editor of the *Tenerife Gazette*. To my surprise and delight, in October 1992 it was published with my photos. 'Ticket to Walk' in the Cañadas and 'Ticket to Fly' followed soon after. From then on writing spurred me to learn Spanish so that I could discover and write more about the island.

I soon discovered that if I told the airhostess that I had the flying equivalent to a GCSE certificate, a Private Pilot's Licence, the Captain might invite me into the cockpit late in the flight. If I passed inspection then I'd be allowed to stay for the landing in Tenerife. Travelling with the excellent Excalibur Airline, I heard Captain Robert Dilworth not only give the best talks to passengers that I had heard but also, during the flight, he allowed wide-eyed children, accompanied by parents, into the cockpit. I guessed, correctly, that he might be willing to help me with 'Ticket to Fly'. He told me about a commercial pilot's approach to landing here and he even offered to proof read my article. With Oscar Martinez, now the airport's Director, I'd had a most informative tour around Tenerife South Airport and the control tower. I admired the new departure signs, the plans for better seating areas and for separating passengers arriving from those departing; these improvements were made.

The night before a return flight with Excalibur, I went to Graham Gold. Singers have a fund of ways both to give their voices a rest and to entertain their customers.

A popular method was to ask questions, "How many of you are from Wales/Ireland/Scotland/Norway?"

Graham was about to sing when he saw me enter the bar and he said, "Ladies and gentlemen, here comes a lady who is a pilot, she could be flying you home.....".

I couldn't disagree. I had to smile and to go along with the flow. Graham flew a micro-light and we had talked about flying.

Next day, on entering the Excalibur plane, I asked the air hostess if by any chance Robert Dilworth was the Captain. He was. Immediately she went to tell him and I was called into the cockpit to receive a warm welcome.

He said, "Leave your things in the overhead compartment and come back for takeoff."

Once in straight and level flight I returned to my seat and I got some very odd looks from the couple beside me. After a few minutes they could restrain themselves no longer.

"Were you at the bar where Graham Gold was singing last night?" they asked.

"Yes," I replied.

"Well, why aren't you in the cockpit flying this plane?" they queried.

Sadly, Excalibur 'went bust' in 1996.

Chapter 13
Guaguas – buses

With the wisdom of hindsight, I realise that getting older has not brought me prudence. I knew that hot weather was incompatible with eczema and allergy to my own sweat, but the stunning beauty and purity of the air at El Teide National Park, combined with small family atmosphere of the 342 bus ride, caught me in its spell. Thanks to the real Tenerife, away from the touristic coastline, and my urge to explore, I have found stalwart friends and accumulated copious happy memories.

Local transport was as good as any service can be that is affected by the vagaries of visitors. Most of the TITSA drivers did their repetitive job with an incredible amount of patience, despite being faced by the same questions in a variety of languages every time the bus door opened.

A visitor asked, "Where ya goin' mate?"

Adeje always received some inventive pronunciations such as, "Do you go to Adedge-ee?"

An experienced driver answered, in Spanish, "Yes and this bus goes to Adekee as well"; only the locals appreciated his joke.

However, of all the nationalities, it was the Italians who reigned supreme at demolishing the TITSA timetable. My heart fell when I saw them at the bus stop, standing out like beacons in their smart outfits liberally sprinkled with gold, as though they had just emerged from a Gucci shop. A crowded bus with standing room only, and already 20 minutes late, was delayed a further 9 minutes while an Italian tried a wallet full of useless BONOs - discount tickets - in the bus's machine before admitting defeat. He paid in cash! Italians were always in pairs, but they sat separately at window seats and conversed loudly - while the other passengers cringed!

The majority of my bus rides were between Los Cristianos and Las Américas and usually I travelled on the 487 (now 488) Airport bus with either Martín or Eugenio. They worked approximately 0700-1500hrs or 1500-2300hrs and soon they recognised me. Once I'd learned some Spanish, they asked about the UK and, when I didn't understand, I could see these kind men trying to think of an easier way to say something. It was thanks to them, and to Cristina, that my language skills began to improve.

I'd found Cristina in TITSA's tiny office in Pueblo Canario, Las Américas. With incredible patience, she endured work conditions that shocked me. Without 'services', she stood all day answering visitors' questions, counting and bagging the bus drivers' money; after work she carried it, often unaccompanied, to the bank deposit across the road! Cristina's kindness, in chatting with me over a fruit juice in the nearby bar during her brief rest break, was way beyond her call of duty. At first, our conversation in Spanish lasted five minutes, but eventually came the great day when we spoke no English. I suspect that, despite her fluency in four languages and her ability to interpret a foreigner's version of Spanish, she must have found our chats hard work.

Only once, when I'd booked a three-week Spanish course in the north of Tenerife, did I travel daily, often with the same driver, the 50-mile each way journey to Santa Cruz, the capital of Tenerife. After a drunk-disturbed sleep I caught the 0700hrs bus from Las Américas, had a 20-minute walk at the other end. I arrived exhausted just before classes began at 0900hrs; they ended at 1300hrs. By then the sun had spread blowtorch strength heat around the Santa Cruz bus station and sensibly most passengers waited in the shade until the bus arrived.

But I stood sweating at the bus stop in the blazing sun. I had to be first in the queue to get a seat at the front of the bus to avoid head pains caused by the draughts from open windows. I was scratching furiously when a kind driver, Fernando Berravente, recognised me and took me to his bus which was parked in the shade. There he told me about himself. He'd been a professional boxer, was a Mormon, had a wife and two children and he gave me a recipe to help eczema – all before he drove to the bus stop to collect his passengers.

I've kept no record of the numerous enjoyable bus rides that I've had in the 342 bus to El Teide with Arcadio Gonzalez García. Somehow, despite only speaking Spanish, he made passengers feel welcome; the atmosphere in his bus was always congenial. He had a great sense of humour. When I asked him where he was taking his bottom (culo), instead of bucket (cubo), he laughed and told me that he collected waste food for his dogs from the restaurants at El Portillo. He'd even built a frame in the luggage space beneath the bus so the bucket wouldn't spill.

Eventually my Spanish improved sufficiently to not only speak to him but, harder still, to understand him. He was possibly the most internationally famous driver working for TITSA; he received cards

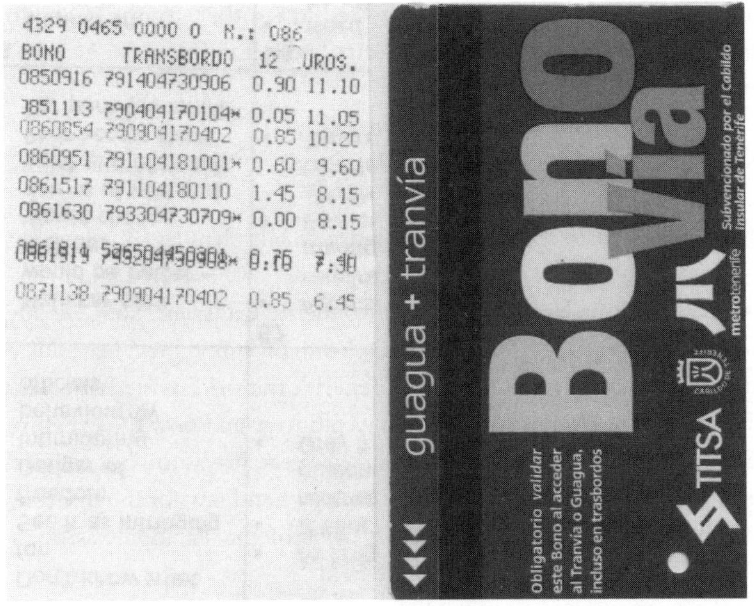

TITSA's BONO discount ticket

A BONO ticket is cheaper than paying money for a return ticket. Insert the BONO into the machine with the colour side facing you and with arrows pointing down.

from a world-wide fan club. Arcadio started working for Transportes de Tenerife in March 1966 when buses had a driver and a conductor. A year later the company became TITSA and, like many other drivers, he'd moved from Güimar to Adeje for work. He was not the only famous member of his family. In 1998 his beautiful, clever daughter Emilía (Mili) not only was elected Miss Tenerife but also she put her physics degree to good use, to present the weather on Canarian TV.

When Arcadio used the word 'reclamación' I was confident that he was telling me that I could ask for a refund. I went expectantly to Cristina who explained that it meant 'reclaim, refund and complaint'. Someone had written a reclamación about Arcadio's unscheduled photograph stop on the road to the Cañadas. I decided to redress the balance. Every business, bar and restaurant had a complaint book and successively numbered pages had extra copies underneath. It was essential to use this because writing a letter of complaint, as we do in the UK, usually would be ignored. The bus station's complaint book had a copy, I kept one and I posted the other to the Cabildo, Department of Transport in Santa Cruz. Sadly it did not save Arcadio's initiative.

But his humour never disappeared.

A Spanish lady complained to him, saying, "You shouldn't talk to passengers when you are driving."

His immediate response was, "Better to talk than to fall asleep."

It was at the Cañadas that I met two wonderful Canarian ladies. By July, the ugly, ground-hugging medusa's head of spiky grey leaves had erupted into the glorious symbol of Tenerife, the red Tajinste Rojo. This tall candle of red florets had flaunted its plumage and now the excessive heat was demolishing its glory for another year. It was too hot to walk, and I was wondering how to fill five hours when I saw for the first time that the door of the tiny chapel in front of the Parador was open. Obviously a service was about to be held.[1]

Coaches parked and unloaded their passengers; 90% of them were ladies and all spoke Spanish. Those who could not squeeze into the building snuggled into the shade in the entrance and I too stayed by the

---

[1] Regular Sunday services are held now, weather permitting.

door to watch the altar being prepared with roses and wheat. Eventually a priest arrived and members of the congregation, including the lady next to me, contributed to the service. Afterwards I spoke to her and, when the procession circled the building, she took my arm and we followed. I exchanged addresses with Eugenia Roncero and her friend, Miguelina Baucells.

On my first visit to Eugenia's home I was surprised that immediately she whisked me off in a taxi to the hospital. Here her friend Miquelina introduced me to her seriously ill husband; he wrote for the newspaper, *El Día*. Bravely he managed a few words before having to return to the oxygen and we did not stay long. I was so sorry that our first meeting was in such sad circumstances; he died soon after and the condolences in *El Día* were many.

I have been honoured to enjoy the loyal and understanding friendship and company of Miguelina and Eugenia. They knew that I had been looking for a second-hand edition of *Natura y Cultura*, a book described as 'a bible of information about Tenerife'. Eugenia told me that a new edition was available and before I found the bookshop this gentle, generous lady presented me with a copy – a Christmas present

Arcadio, the El Teide bus driver for many years

from them both. After she lost her brave battle with cancer, Eugenia was sorely missed by her family and by all her many friends.

When Arcadio told me that there would soon be a new museum beside the Parador, I went to look; it wasn't open, but I was thrilled when two ladies who had been cleaning the area invited me to share their lunch. After years of believing that I was a linguistic failure, to begin to understand the Canarians never ceased to amaze me. If I'd not made the effort to learn Spanish I'd have missed a lot of fun. Sitting on the entrance floor near the new toilets, I was the recipient of spontaneous Canarian hospitality. We used the delicious fresh bread to scoop up the last juices of the salad. Shortly afterwards my article 'And it didn't cost a penny' was published.

Whenever I wanted a walk without an early start, I explored the hills nearby and one day I was surprised to hear voices. Immediately I went to investigate. In front of a cave near the edge of the barranco, a family was seated at tables; they insisted that I join them and drink a glass of their local wine. A year later, on 1st May, a fiesta when they celebrated the Day of the Workers, I walked uphill to a deserted village where the ruined houses sat comfortably on the crest of a ridge. Although many of the stone walls were crumbling, those still intact were a glorious mixture of shapes and colours.

An old man, I later learned his name was Cixto, pointed to a path I'd not done before. It crossed the barranco giving me a different descent route and, on reaching the other side, I recognised my surroundings. I was near the cave. Here again I met the family, Blanca, a teacher, her husband Hucho and their daughter María. They invited me to visit their house in Guía de Isora and here she introduced me to her friend Pili. I was thrilled to meet these kind Canarians but, because of the speed and the volume of their conversation, at first our meetings were exhausting.

Then Blanca generously invited me to join them and their friends for Sundays at their cave in the delightfully peaceful El Chorro; it did wonders for my Spanish. Early in the morning the men worked on the land tending the vines and doing other chores. At about 1100hrs, Blanca, her mother Maruka, María, and anyone else who could be squeezed into the transport were driven up the steep dusty track; later it was tarmaced thanks to local agricultural grants.

Their terrace had a sink with natural hot water, heated by the volcano, that came direct from the mountain's water galleries. There was even a proper toilet. However, everything had to be locked because passing walkers had used a small open cave area for toilet purposes! While the men started cooking we helped ourselves to fresh bread, local cheese and the excellent local wine from the Guía cooperative. There followed a procession of good food, meat and Canarian potatoes or a huge paella cooked on an enormous barbecue area. The meal always ended with strong coffee and, on 28th February, Hucho's birthday was shared with his friend Fílix and another man. Each year our numbers increased until by the 90th birthday of Hucho's father, Santiago, there were over forty of us.

All my efforts to learn Spanish were worthwhile when a surprised Fílix said, "She understood my joke."

It was when walking near Chio, not far from Guía, that on 1st March I'd been stung by bees. The weather conditions from Africa, called La Calima, had arrived and with them came an unpleasant heat, 30°C or above, air with varying density of dust and sometimes a severely vicious wind. If the nearby island of La Gomera looked hazy, not its usual knife-sharp clear outline, then the Calima was here. For locals, for those involved in agriculture and not least for asthmatics, La Calima proved that hot weather was *not* always good weather. When I mentioned my bee stings to Hucho he laughed. He owned the bees. Then his voice became serious as he explained that here bees' *unprovoked* aggression *does* increase in direct proportion to the rise in temperature.

Those of us from Northern Europe are bought up to think that if we leave bees alone, then the bees won't attack us. But here in the Canary Islands, in hot weather, it is *definitely* wise to avoid areas signed '*colmenas peligroso*', beehives danger. Hucho moved his hives from Chio to the Cañadas between 15th April and 31st August; recently the maximum number of hives allowed in the park was 4,179 and every hive position was recorded. Pollination not only helped the plants; the bees gave me some consolation for my stings because from Blanca's father, Martín, I bought some superb honey.

Then tragedy struck. Within a year, Blanca lost both her father, Martín, and her husband and these memorable days came to a sudden end. But here friends made are never forgotten and Pili achieved a standard of spoken English that puts my Spanish to shame.

1400hrs on Saturdays was a dangerous time to be on the roads. Canarian men were driving home for lunch and the speed and steadiness of some drivers gave cause for concern. But the 342 bus was not due until 1630hrs and I was stranded between Escalona and Arona. It was thanks to the *absence* of a bus that the barman introduced me to Lorenzo, who offered to take me to Arona. He drove perfectly so I took the opportunity to ask him about the horses that I had seen at village fiestas. Lorenzo gave me his phone number so that if his friend Melinge agreed, I could visit him and his horses.

This I did. I was glad that Melinge Fumero understood my allergy, he knew people with this problem and after a brief introduction to Sabina, a ravishing brunette, and Airosa, a six-year-old grey, we sat outside the stable. As I enjoyed a glass of his excellent wine, he told me that both animals worked for their keep by helping to cultivate the ground that provided their fodder, maize, alfalfa, carrots and Canarian millet. I was surprised that in the Municipio of Arona there were about 500 horses and that the numbers were similar in villages throughout Tenerife. Sadly I had to refuse his wonderful offer of a ride in el campo. Later I realised that on this small island Lorenzo knowing Melinge was not luck. Soon after I'd met Lorenzo I told a bus driver how I'd met Melinge and he replied, laughing, "Melinge is the cousin of my wife".

It was with José Luis Gonzalez - who, with his wife Carlota, had stayed with me in Bangor - that I went rock climbing at Arico. Resembling the UK's sandstone outcrops, very short, steep and fingery with smooth rounded footholds, it was like trying to stand on a sloping ledge covered in ball bearings. It was a great day out but, despite my good climbing technique, my arms were weak and I managed only a couple of routes - with a rope twanging tight! Most climbs were Grade 5 and above, and were best suited to the stick-insect bodies of twenty year olds.

What impressed me most was the superb choice of activities available for local people's recreation – on water, in the air (hang gliding) or on terra firma. The excellent climate rarely curtailed any sporting activity and while I was astounded that the majority of visitors came here only to sunbathe, few had strayed away from the coastline, it had left unspoiled the tiny hamlets in the hills. The original Canarian single-storied houses had small windows with shutters to keep out both heat and cold. Only an occasional grotesque large-windowed, two-story house surrounded by high fences retaining barking dogs assaulted the delightful scenery.

Often friends in the UK asked, "Why are *you* going *there*?"

I had the answer.

Without the help of José Luis, the difficulties of a two-night visit to the nearby tiny island of El Hierro would have defeated me. This kind man drove me the 60 miles (97kms) to Los Rodeos airport in the north, for take off at 0840hrs on Tuesday 28th June; travel was cheaper midweek. Once settled into a small hotel in Valverde, my priority was to arrange the car hire for the following day. I'd never driven in the Canary Islands before so I wanted a car that was familiar to me, and without a missing wheel nut as had happened in Cyprus! At home I drove a red Ford Escort. The hire firm had one the same colour and with only 37 miles (60km) on the clock!

After all was arranged I went for a walk and was surprised when two cars stopped; both were driven by single men who asked me if I needed a lift. I refused but when the next car stopped the old lady, Mrs Pedrona Pieras, immediately got out and held her seat forward. This wonderful retired couple were returning from a visit to a hospital nearby and they insisted that I went with them to their home in Mochanal for lunch. Their garden was a riot of colour and it was obvious that it received a lot of love and attention. Soon egg and chips was served together with some excellent local wine. Although my Spanish was improving, communication for both of us was a challenge. While we drank our coffee I saw their family album and it was with regret that I left this spontaneous, generous couple.

On both Christmas and New Year's Day supermarkets were open in the morning and the buses provided a Sunday timetable, but with a slightly later start. However, Christmas Eve, Noche Buena, was the one night in the year when the bus service closed down early, by 2000hrs, so that families could gather together for a sumptuous meal. Anyone who got stuck miles away from their base could face impressive battles for the few taxis.

On my first Christmas Day in Tenerife I went with Arcadio to the

Cañadas, and as usual passengers were soon talking to each other. The sky was a brilliant blue, the sun was warm and a slight chill in the wind was sufficient to prevent sweating. When we'd passed the García rocks and reached the largest cave, we could sit below ground level, out of the wind. I remembered meeting a local here who told me that when he'd put an unlit cigarette on the rock a lizard had snatched it and disappeared. The first rustle of paper alerts opportunistic lizards that emerge from every nook and cranny. In the warmer months they had a tug of war with a piece of banana skin, explored my rucksack and even sunbathed on my knee.

Christmas 1996 was very special. Not only was it my first Christmas in Adeje but also Martín, the kind airport bus driver with a voice that would melt butter in Antarctica, invited me to his home for Noche Buena. Martín collected me after work at 2100hrs and in San Isidro I met his wife, Tonia, three children aged sixteen, fourteen and five, his mother and sister, her husband and baby and cousins. We ate a procession of good things and it was all wonderfully informal.

By 2330hrs bed was organised and I understood why we were not going to church. On Christmas Day Tonia worked from 0600-1200hrs and 1800-0430hrs yet they found time to accept a stranger into their home *and* to cope with my low-level, non-Canarian Spanish. The next morning was spent eating, talking and watching some TV and after lunch Tonia went for a well-earned rest. Martín took me back to my apartment before he started work at 1500hrs.

With a few hours of daylight left I was desperately in need of a little exercise and the quiet path leading to Taucho was drenched in the warmth of the afternoon sun. After a lung-stretching uphill walk I was pondering whether it was sensible to turn back when I heard voices and spotted a couple descending. The man was Irish, his friend was German and we chatted during the descent.

In their two-week visit this enterprising pair had put the time to good use. It was unusual to meet a couple who, on their first visit to Tenerife, had stayed in the quietest villages in the south. They'd had four nights in both Masca and in Vilaflor, walked up Guajara, the third highest mountain and they had endured some disturbed nights in an apartment above a noisy bar in Los Gigantes.

On this Christmas Day, they said that they had nowhere to stay, so it seemed appropriate to invite this adventurous couple to use my spare room for their last two nights. After inspecting the apartment, doubtless for decibel levels, they accepted. A lot seemed to have been packed into the 24 hours since Martín had taken me to his home. I went to bed happy on Christmas night, knowing that I had been able to follow his lead and offer hospitality on this special day - even if I slept little with strangers nearby!

Chapter 14
Learning Spanish

It was thanks to a timeshare salesman whose office was in my complex, Pueblo Torviscas, that I took my first tentative steps to try to learn Spanish. He was late for our appointment and I'd decided to wait no longer.

I wrote, 'I have waited 15 minutes and that is as long as I wait for any man.'

I was trying to put this note on my apartment door when he arrived, took it, read it, laughed and our chat began. David McKelvey had been a pilot and we even knew people in common in Wales. After he'd showed me the apartments for 'sale', not only did he let me avoid the strong timeshare sales pitch that always followed, but also he gave me a bottle of champagne for going on the tour.

It was Heather, the girl friend of David's colleague, who summed me up well.

As she loaned me '*Linkword Spanish*' she said, "Don't dismiss it, try it."

Despite grave doubts about my skills, this book opened a door that I never thought I'd succeed in unlocking, to talk to local people. Thanks to clever planning, few words per page, plenty of repetition and simple, attainable goals, it succeeded where others had not. I devoured most of the nouns and the few verbs.

What really impressed me, a cynical, retired teacher, was the book's approach to learning the male and female nouns: 'the bull is pretty' (*el* tor*o* esta bonit*o*), 'the cow is pretty' (*la* vac*a* esta bonit*a*). Unusual phrases helped me to remember the words rather than guess them by association,'a red cow eats a window' (la vaca roja come la ventana). At first I could get by with only two verbs and two tenses:'I have' (tengo) 'you have' (tiene),'I want' (quiero) and 'you want' (quiere). When I left my glasses on the 342 Teide bus, I knew the word 'gafas' and next day I collected them from the bus office.

At first my tentatively used few words in Spanish were not understood and, when they were, all too often the response included many words that I didn't know. I turned for help to the author of *Linkword Spanish*, University Psychology Lecturer Dr Michael Gruneberg. Sadly he had no plans for a book 2 and, to progress further, a course seemed to be the only solution.

A fluent Spanish speaker told me that in summer the one, two or three month courses at Salamanca University had a superb reputation, comparable with Oxford and Cambridge. A recommendation like this was appreciated because I'd heard about some less than honourable language schools that operated in the UK. I booked a one month course in September 1992. To get the best value from the cost of my travel and accommodation I chose 5 hours' study per day.

For the first two hours, 0900-1100hrs, Consuelo taught grammar brilliantly *only* in Spanish to a cosmopolitan group from Belgium, France, Japan and me. With zero time allowed to move to another building, we rushed to the language lab at 1100hrs and then to a vocabulary class at 1200hrs. Because the light in my bedroom, both in daytime and at night, was insufficient to do any homework, every day I took a packed lunch - cheese, bread roll without butter, an apple and a biscuit - to a park nearby. Here I worked hard, weighing down my papers when it was windy and the time passed surprisingly quickly. The conversation class began at 1700hrs. Sometimes we stayed in one bar and on other days it became a Spanish tapas crawl. Tapas were small tasty morsels of food, which were washed down by a drink at each bar. I enjoyed the choice of food but I never managed to empty my glass before we moved on.

With an intense level of concentration needed in class and constant walking from place to place, I found the course tough going. It wasn't helped by my tripping on a pavement edge, 'turning' my ankle on the second day and making every step very painful. My hosts spoke no

English and at meal times the sympathetic mother tried to ask me questions, but rarely could I answer her. However, their diet was everything I didn't eat. The evening meal was greasy chips with a fried egg (the hollows of the whites were filled with oil) fried potato cake (potato, onion and egg) or fish in batter. The student hostel food was similar so it was no surprise that a large number of us suffered from upset stomachs.

The father was a policeman and the family's television was monopolised by football, the Pink Panther and other cartoons. Evenings were difficult until a week of fiesta fun and entertainment brought some memorable new experiences. One night the surface of the magnificent Plaza Mayor was covered with black and white squares to become a chessboard. The straight-backed king sat proudly on his horse, the queen moved regally and a man with a megaphone shouted the instructions for the moves from a balcony above them.

On another evening I was fascinated by the speed and efficiency of the 24 models who were displaying a variety of glamorous furs. Twelve were out of sight, changing. With immaculate timing, as soon as six models were descending from the stage while removing their furs (to the delight of men trying to get glimpses of the revealing body stocking underneath), another six were coming onto the stage. The girls could have been clones. They all had long legs, tanned skin, very dark hair drawn back into a vertical roll at the back of their head and the popular dangling strand of hair hung in front of every left ear.

Most impressive was Salamanca itself. It was an architectural paradise. I kept returning to the Casa de Las Conchas, the house with shell walls that was started in 1493, completed in 1517 and declared a National Monument in 1929. With two cathedrals, one built in the 12-13th centuries and the other in the 16th century, the place was a feast of culture. In September the sun was pleasantly warm, but not fierce, so I could enjoy exploring Salamanca's many nooks and crannies. At weekends there were well-organised excursions that cost extra. Only in Escorial did I admit defeat. Spending twenty minutes in front of each picture listening to fast, incomprehensible Spanish was non-survivable. I left them to it. For a Spanish learner, infinitely preferable would have been more time to explore the superb old town of Ávila. By the end of the course my brain was overflowing, yet no words would come out of my mouth, so I missed the splendid opportunity to practise my Spanish with the old men, who regularly sat in the Plaza Mayor hoping for a chat.

When staying in Bill's studio, I went everywhere with a dictionary and a notebook so that I could record every new word. Some, such as 'Jueves' (Thursday) were more difficult to remember than others and these were transferred from notebook to notebook until I remembered them. It was comforting to hear that other learners' memories also failed with 'Jueves'. On every bus journey I learned something new. When a driver shouted 'Gomera' out of the window at inconsiderate female motorists (and 'Gomero' to male drivers) I thought that a surprising number of drivers knew a lot of people from La Gomera. Calling someone 'Gomero' was not a compliment!

I felt that my rate of improvement was incompatible with the number of years that I might have left, so when Cristina told me about a three-week language course in Santa Cruz in July I decided to go. The huge numbers studying at Salamanca had enabled the University to divide students, from beginners to advanced standard, into compatible groups, with many classes at each level. In Santa Cruz, however, there were a total of about twenty students in two classes. The inevitable result was that the ability of the students in both the classes varied enormously.

No doubt because of the daily 50-mile journey each way, I can remember little about the lessons that ended at 1330hrs. Sometimes there was an excursion starting at 1700hrs, after their siesta break, to various places of interest on the island. I went only once because not only did I have to wait in a park un-rested, un-washed and without a change of clothes, but also to return south I had to leave the group after a couple of hours and before they went to eat!

From then on I decided that structured courses can get you only so far. It was time to concentrate my energies on conversation with anyone who had time to chat – usually bus drivers or retired folk in the countryside. The National Park offered free guided walks around El Portillo, but booking a walk had to be done ahead by phoning the park office. This I did, explaining in Spanish that I'd arrive at El Portillo, at 1115hrs in the 342 bus. Twice a guide was not there to meet me so I presumed that my poor Spanish had caused a misunderstanding; I did the easy linear walk to La Fortalezza, recommended by the staff manning the park's centre, that fitted conveniently with the bus times.

Eventually I met a charming young park guide, José Ramón Flores, whose impressive preparation included maps and other aids to support his fascinating information. It was difficult to comprehend that, millions of years ago, a massive volcano had exploded and the flat floor of the Cañadas and another 'happening' had created two levels. The lower section, Ucanca, towards the south, was divided from the higher northern part by the line of the García rocks, opposite the Parador. I was surprised and relieved that José spoke good English and only at the end of our walk did he admit why he'd been reluctant to go with me.

I was ashamed when he said, "Some British people had complained about the standard of my English."

To ensure that I got the front seat on all the journeys to the stunning Cañadas with Arcadio, I waited at the first bus stop in Las Américas. Often by talking to him I met other Spanish speakers. Maite, a charming lady from San Sebastián, had a boyfriend, Jonathan, from mid-Wales; they visited me in Bangor and we kept in touch for some years.

Then one day Arcadio asked, "Have you been to the summit of El Teide?"

"No," I replied.

He suggested that I took the cable car up El Teide because queues were not as long as usual, the wind was light and the visibility was perfect; I raided my pocket for a return ride. From the top station, the 531ft (162m) walk up to the summit crater was on steep, rough, rocky ground. Valiantly struggling up this path was a procession of coach passengers whose body sizes, shapes, ages, and footwear guaranteed that many of them were severely challenged by the terrain and the altitude. Despite their being watched on every step by a vigilant park guide seated near the summit, I wondered what they'd do if anyone had fainted on this path.

Other than warnings about altitude at the bottom station, to anyone with heart and other problems, safety on this final part of the ascent seemed minimal. A guide blew a whistle to attract attention before shouting instructions to stay on the path, in four languages, to

The El Teide teleférico's new aerodynamic cable car

anyone who strayed an inch from it. At the crater, heat warmed those standing near to the rocks, the smell of sulphur was strong and the views were superb. It was money well spent! My lungs, that disliked the UK's pollened and polluted air in summer, appreciated the pure Cañadas air. I could walk up steep hillsides and dig deep into parts of my lungs that all too often were closed down to defend themselves against irritants. Today, the final ascent is controlled; with a passport and its photocopies, prior permission can to be obtained from the National Park Office.

To find a person with the standard of English that was roughly the same level as my Spanish, for a more structured one-to-one conversation, was a challenge. Where could I find this 'someone'? The people who knew me in reception were too busy to cope with my faltering Spanish and the Canarians in the countryside seemed to speak with an accent as difficult to understand as some British accents. On a 'can't lose, might win' basis, I put an advertisement in a local language school asking for someone to do 'intercambio'. Ideally this would be speaking half an hour in English and half an hour in Spanish. I was so lucky.

Mari Cabrera, a charming lady, contacted me. She worked in the busy office of her brother Marcos, an Assesoria Fiscal (tax adviser), in Los Cristianos. We were amazed how often if one of us said a word in her language, the other could guess the meaning correctly - the word 'menopause' led to a long and detailed exchange of information! I missed both her good company and help with my Spanish when her family commitments meant that our meetings had to stop.

The last place I expected to have any language practice was in an English bar called Liverpool Lou, where Karen, with classic Liverpudlian humour, and her Spanish boyfriend, Greg, always gave me a lovely welcome. I was amazed when I walked in one evening to hear Greg talking to a young Canarian, small in stature, dangerously circular of girth, drunk but under control. It was as incongruous as classical music being played in bars here, but, in keeping with my policy to practise my Spanish at every opportunity, I asked him a question. He understood and soon I was being invited to a fiesta in his village, Arona. I hesitated, he gave me his phone number and this gave me time to check his pedigree with Greg.

For some time I'd been trying to find out when and where the fiestas were held, but I'd only heard about them after the event. I phoned him to say 'yes'. Despite warnings about Spanish men's late arrival for dates, he arrived in the bar, near the bus stop in Arona, soon after me. Immediately, with a shocked voice, he questioned why I was drinking a coffee; he had wine then and at every bar afterwards. His friend, Franci (Francine) was a nationalist whose reasons why Tenerife should be independent from Spain were similar to those I had heard in parts of the UK.

On this memorable day, the streets and bars gradually filled and, after the church service, I went to see the procession that included many Arab-looking horses with their proudly arched necks and dancing feet. Their riders kept them under tight control but I avoided their rear ends, not for the obvious reason but for two others. Without a red reversing warning light, unexpectedly and rapidly they would go backwards and, despite the purity of Canarian air, in the very narrow streets, my lungs complained about the proximity of horses. Afterwards, we went to a line of tables laden with tempting food.[1] The beans were

[1] Now food is served from carts during the street procession.

El Teide National Park

As visitor numbers increased, the belt of controls tightened. To walk to the

hot and tasty and the local cheese and figs were superb, the latter being covered with a white sugary powder. And all this was in a perfect setting; the backcloth was El Conde hill, looking impressive in the sunshine.

He was a good host and, despite some serious drinking all around us, I saw no unpleasant, drunken behaviour. Music issued forth from bars, from the rooftops, La Azotea, indeed from wherever groups gathered. Some tunes I could describe only as mournful dirges, but others were lovely, jolly and foot-tapping. Obviously this would go on well into the evening because families do not eat their evening meal until 2100hrs, or after. Every village celebrated two saints' days in a year and today, 17th January, Arona celebrated San Antonio de Abad. Being January, when the temperature went down with the sun, I was grateful to accept Francine's offer of a lift back.

A solo, foreign female, of uncertain age, stood out in the crowd and that day I learned another lesson - that on this island there was no action without reaction! When Arcadio had his rest days, Antonio drove the Teide bus; he lived in Arona and he saw me at the fiesta. Antonio told Arcadio and other bus drivers that I had a boy friend; when, some time later, the 'boyfriend's' name was in the paper, for biting off a piece from a man's ear in a disagreement, the comments of the bus drivers can be imagined.

I liked the village atmosphere where I was surrounded by local people. To find a base where rarely could anyone speak English was now my goal.

Chapter 15
Apartment living

Being an only child and brought up in peaceful rural surroundings it was a new and unpleasant shock to live in an apartment.A pin dropping could wake me up so my sleep depended totally upon the families above, below and beside me.The bonus of life here was that, with the exception of some ex-pat lounges, the cooling floor tiles in Canarian homes were delightfully free from dust-collecting best Wilton carpets and dogs. But I still had to travel with my own bedding, sheets, pillows, duvet and washing powder.

The best thing about Bill's studio in Pueblo Torviscas was the proximity of Stephan's bar. Here I met Alison. She too had sensitive lungs that appreciated Tenerife's clean air and it was thanks to her that I heard about the church situated near the Casino in Las Américas. On Sundays a Roman Catholic service was held at 0900hrs, the Anglican at 1015hrs and the Lutheran at 1200hrs; throughout the winter rarely was a seat empty at any time.Afterwards we went to 'socialise' at the bar nearby for coffee and to meet new people, both residents and 'Swallows' who returned each winter.At the church door, books and really useful 'Just to say' cards were for sale because the church funds came from the collections only.

The studio's worst feature was that the balcony doors - the only source of fresh air - were in direct line-of-sound with noisy bars on the main road a few hundred metres away. Nightly, without fail, from 2100hrs I could hear the singer's every word and, unable to concentrate on a book, I'd read the same line time after time; I was forced to go out.

Hard, plastic seats in bars had to be endured until I could return, bath and be in bed by midnight when the law said that the volume should be lowered and the bar doors closed!

The torture began when my body was aching for sleep but the racket continued after midnight. By the time it ceased I'd accumulated more open sores. Occasionally I'd rise, get dressed and march into the bar where I'd have a loud, stress-releasing row in English with the management. Most customers pretended not to hear my comments or the replies of the bar staff as they tried, forcibly, to remove me from their premises. To make a complaint I was told to go to the local police station in Fañabe and this I did. It challenged my Spanish because few local policemen (I saw no females doing this job either) spoke English. As someone said, "If you don't like noise, don't go to Spain."

Ever hopeful, I requested a quiet room when I booked the course in Salamanca. But on arrival my heart fell when I saw that it was in the centre of a long tiled corridor. I knew immediately that I could not survive there for a night, never mind three weeks. With loud footsteps and many doors to bang throughout the night, disturbed sleep would make life intolerable. Now the only available accommodation that the University could offer me was with a family. Eventually I found their apartment on the ground floor of a huge tower block with a square central hollow surrounded by inward-facing apartment windows. I could not have designed a better way to ensure that neighbours overheard all family discussions. But a pleasant surprise awaited me, I slept well.

However, evenings with the family were an endurance test because the low wattage single light in my room made reading impossible. Only when I moved into the village of Adeje, where I had only Spanish mainland and Canarian TV channels, did I realise that there was a dearth of interesting programmes. After 2100hrs, other than cartoons, two topics seemed to monopolise all the channels. One involved making peace between arguing family members/neighbours, the other was cheap-to-produce TV 'games'. These were accompanied by the well-rehearsed, inane jokes and chatter between a gigolo-type man and a female dolly bird about to fall out of her dress that we see on some programmes in the UK! After the Salamanca experience it seemed a good idea to find and book a decent apartment before I started the course in Santa Cruz in the north of Tenerife. I went in May for a week to do just that.

In July I caught the bus from Tenerife South Airport to Santa Cruz and took a taxi to the apartment, but at Reception a shock greeted me. There was no accommodation available. It was my fault; I'd given them my name, address, everything – except a deposit! They kindly rang a hotel and there I stayed for a night but my window opened onto the central, dark, airless tube that was similar to the one 'outside' my window in Salamanca. If I moved I broke into a sweat and I envied my cheese and melon that I'd brought from the UK the cool of the bedroom's fridge. To stay here was impossible. Now I realised just how meltdown hot it got here in summer.

Back in Torviscas I dumped my bags in the bar with the English owner and after much searching I heard that a lady might have apartments to rent. She worked in a bar in a nearby complex and I was thankful to move into a light, airy top floor apartment, for 4,000 pesetas a night. The very early rising needed to get to the course by 0900hrs wasn't helped by the Roman amphitheatre complex design. It was easy to hop from one balcony to another, and with incredible efficiency it ensured that one noisy group 'enjoying themselves' on their balcony until 0400hrs (there was always one) kept everyone else awake. Survival was tough but worse was to come.

I was preparing a meal one evening when the phone rang in the apartment.

"Who are you?" asked the voice.

"Who are you?" I replied.

It was the owner of the apartment phoning from the UK wondering why I was using it without her knowledge. Another owner must have told her. I had to move out at the end of that week and it being July I was lucky to find another apartment for 7,000 pesetas a night.

Only for my last few days after the course had ended could I relax in Bill Foster's studio, but the heat and the 50-mile each way journey had exhausted me. Then I saw my first mosquito. The windows had to stay open to catch any much-needed movement of air so off went the lights and, hoping that the mosquito would leave, I decided to practise my Spanish with Stephan. On my return my heart fell when I realised that my habit, to pick up the key before leaving, had been replaced by collecting the rubbish bag. There was no spare key in reception and all I wanted was a bath and bed.

Luckily the security guard, Ramón, was on duty. In an earlier visit to Tenerife he had introduced me to a sidewalk caricaturist who offered to draw me. Thanking him I said no, not with my nose and anyway I had no money. However, because it was a quiet evening, he said he'd do it for free, because it would attract other customers. It did.

As he worked, passers-by congregated saying, "OOOH, wait till you see that, luv", and other similar comments. I dreaded the result but, despite a positively penile nose, he had drawn it with such kindness and humour that it was a wonderful, treasured gift.

I was lucky that unlike most second floor apartments, here, my balcony was approachable by climbing across the roof that was accessible from the staircase. At least I'd left the French window half-latched. Ramón was unseen on the far slope of the roof and for a long while nothing happened then came crash after crash. He could not have fallen all those times! Eventually a dusty, dirty Ramón emerged from the front door. He had removed some tiles in the hope of making an entry through the concrete roof before giving up and finally jumping down onto the balcony! His reward was a 'Carajillo', a coffee well laced with brandy. Mine was an impressive invoice for repairs from Bill.

I returned to the UK, more drained of energy than I'd been after any rock climb, to face the immediate painting of my lounge days before my cousins arrived from New Zealand. Two of Grandpa Lunt's brothers had left the UK in the 1800s. I had never met Claire, Beth or Mary who looked so like my father; I did know Dorothy who lived in Zurich with her husband, Ernst. I was alone again when at 0300hrs I woke and was making a cup of tea when I passed out. Next thing I knew I was on the kitchen floor, lying against a radiator. I had no memory of phoning 999 or of getting to the bathroom, where a doctor found me being sick into the wash basin while sitting on the toilet.

The ambulance took me to hospital and eventually, after many months, a neck x-ray showed severely damaged cervical discs. It was a long time before the dizzy spells ceased but the legacy lives on. I can

My spacious apartment in Adeje
Doors, from the right, lead to the staircase, the kitchen, bathroom and back bedroom.

neither look upwards for a long time, nor sit for ages on a sleek modern sofa without a back that rises to head level. My efforts to learn Spanish in a hot climate had left me with a permanent disability. Even with the improved head restraint I dread being shunted by a car behind and suffering whiplash, the most common of all car accident injuries.

It was not long after that I was made 'homeless' when Bill decided to live in his studio. Luckily by then Pam Marchant, who'd introduced me to Tenerife, had told me where I could meet the Swallows' British walking group. I met Londoner Frank Wisby who, with his wife Ivy, had lived in Los Cristianos for some years, and he knew British owners who rented their apartments. For over a year I stayed in different accommodation every time I went to Tenerife, which by now was four times a year. Some apartments had better facilities and the likelihood of undisturbed sleep than others, but all too often I suffered from the extensive range of inconsiderate, selfish behaviour perpetrated by those on holiday 'enjoying themselves'.

Well after midnight the click of the pool balls and comments of the players on the terrace below echoed efficiently around one complex. Disturbed sleep occurred in all apartments on the nights before and after British flight days, Tuesdays and Fridays. The clickety click of suitcase wheels running over tiled surfaces gave warning of imminent heavy footsteps and voices resounding above, below or beside me. I could stand it no longer. After four years I looked for a miracle, a quiet apartment to rent all the year, so that I could come and go as I pleased. The bonus would be leaving my bedding and other essentials in Tenerife to make travel easier.

It was thanks to Cristina that I found a minute, one-bedroom apartment conveniently situated in Avenida Suecia in the centre of Los Cristianos. Having read newspaper accounts of the dangers of gas bottles, I was glad that it was safely outside in the courtyard below. However my first-ever three month summer stay in Tenerife began with two problems. Before going to bed I always had a relaxing warm bath before massaging calming creams into wherever they were needed. I hated showers because, even when they functioned properly (many don't), warming one part of the body at a time was hard work.

Although I had tested the taps before moving in, the hot water system failed on my first night. A plumber was found, no mean feat. He sorted it out, but next time I returned again there was no hot water. This time a different man told the landlady that the water heater was illegal and to repair it would lose him his licence. A very unhappy owner (she always said, "Soy pauvre", "I'm poor") had a new heater installed. But a solution to this hot and airless second-floor bedroom was harder to solve. Luckily, onto the floor of the tiny lounge, between the sofa and the wall, I could fit a single mattress, just. At night, by keeping open the lounge window, the apartment door and the landing window, which looked onto the street, a whisker of air current passed over me.

The indoor temperature of the apartment was too hot for me to wash sheets in the bath and I was very grateful for the use of Frank and Ivy Wisby's washing machine.

When he was young, Londoner Frank and his friends did dangerous things such as swimming under barges in the Thames - until three friends failed to return to the surface! Frank says that his father grabbing hold of his hair, while giving him a clout, caused his quiff. The quiff is still there, as is his wife Ivy; in 2006 they celebrated 60 years of marriage!

Either it was sleeping on the floor, or the debilitating heat, or both, but I acquired a crippling back pain. On the worst day I could not get up from the floor and I was very lucky that Elaine Morgan, a friend from the Swallows, found me and bought some painkillers from the nearby pharmacy. Eventually, very slowly, with help, I descended the stairs and went to a bar nearby for some much-needed soup. As well as the back pain and the itching, a severe herpes virus started in one eye making life very unpleasant. For some years I became a regular patient of the excellent eye specialists, but I'd already lost much sight in that eye.

It was while waiting in an eye clinic that I witnessed a classic case of unfortunate behaviour. On a warm but wet, drizzly day, an apparition in full trouser and top waterproofs strode purposefully past the entrance to the eye department.

Seconds later this tall man returned, found Reception and, while tapping his watch on an extended arm, he said, "I'm Major X and I have an appointment at 1100hrs."

My appointment was for 1115hrs and this clinic was notorious for

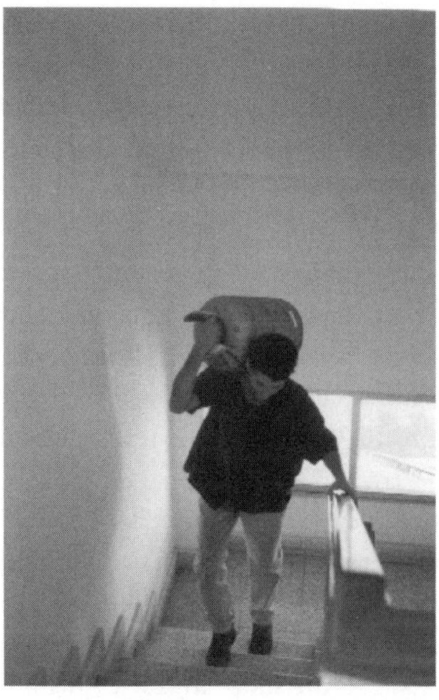

The replacement gas bottle arrives

running late. I was wondering how long his patience would last when I was called in before him.

While I was with the doctor, a nurse entered through an internal door and said, "Major X is complaining about having to wait."

The doctor's reply was, "If he doesn't like our system, he can go elsewhere."

He wasn't there when I left.

I was glad to be free from the UK's summer pollen and the associated need to use steroid inhalers in eyes, nose and lungs but I needed a miracle, a cooler apartment. Then I heard rumours that my landlady and her family had sold the valuable land next door for a healthy sum. The windows of my kitchen and lounge overlooked the small, single story old house where her brother lived. Without doubt soon a four-story building would take its place. No way could I stay here.

Arcadio told me that a German lady was selling her top-floor, one bedroom apartment in Adeje so I went to see it. Sadly it was not in the old, original part of Adeje with its village atmosphere and a 'heart'. It was in the area where new development was eating up ground at an impressive pace. I'd checked that all her previous year's bills had been paid, when I remembered that, during my climbing years in the Alps, Germans, rather than any other nationality, had bought property in the best niches. So when the lady said, "I think it is time to be getting out of Adeje", although I was sure that buying now would be financially beneficial, I never bought, then or later.

Below my lounge window the noise and dust of construction work had started and I'd watched in horror a man balanced precariously on the upturned lip of an excavator's scoop. With his hand below his saw, and at full stretch, he was attacking the wire cable from which hung a block. I held my breath. Just in time he realised the danger and placed his hand above the saw!

Both Arona and Adeje were at about 1100ft (350m) and they were divided by El Conde, a hill from which a cloud often poured towards Adeje leaving Arona in sunshine. Could a giant be sitting on the summit puffing a huge pipe? I chose Adeje.

My frequent visits to the shops in Adeje's main street – the source of most information about accommodation and much else – were fruitless until I met an English girl who lived in the village. Four days before my return to the UK she told me that tenants in her building were moving out of an apartment – but it would be too big for me.

"Tell me more," was my immediate reply.

Her answer was, "It's an attico that faces the Plaza."

I went immediately to speak to the owners who told me to return on Monday. Not having learned from my previous experience, I was walking away when I bumped into her in the street.

"Have you paid a deposit?" she asked.

On hearing that I hadn't, her immediate response was, "Go back and pay it immediately or the apartment won't be there on Monday."

With this lucky encounter on 1st March 1996, with a payment of 15,000 pesetas (250 Euros) deposit, began my journey to some wonderful new experiences. The day before my return to the UK, I saw the spacious lounge, separate kitchen, bathroom and the two bedrooms between which was an area big enough to be a child's play area. It was good to be decadent with space and the advantage was that I could avoid the afternoon sun that poured into the lounge. The apartment was being painted, the front door's cylinder lock was being changed and there was a separate, lockable washroom on the terrace opposite my door. Locals who'd been born and brought up here lived nearby and even though tourism was not far away, the atmosphere was all that I'd hoped for, that of a Canarian village.

As with the previous apartment I returned for a 'test run' for two weeks in May, prior to the pollen-avoiding three months in summer, and history repeated itself. The hot water system didn't work until the owner's cousin, or others, had time to solve the problem. Luckily I didn't know that this saga would continue until 2002 when a new water heater was installed.

The water here was full of calcium and, without modern improvements, gradually the internal diameter of the piping had been reduced. So for my nightly bath I turned on the hot water tap, waited for it to run warm then put in the plug. Once I'd turned off the tap I could get no more hot water because it ran cold before more hot water emerged. As for the toilet, it was unique. In the centre of the cistern's lid was a knob to pull but persistently it disconnected from its connection below. For some years I removed the lid, did it manually and explained this 'idiosyncrasy' to any visitors. I was very glad when this, and a problem with the oven, was solved. But, despite these annoyances, the position of the apartment was superb. It was a case of 'if you don't like football, don't go to the match!'

Now that I had only Spanish television channels, my suspicions were confirmed; a high percentage of programmes were unwatchable dross. Even the news at 2000hrs had innumerable reporters rooted to the spot speaking into a microphone at a phenomenal rate of knots. But commentaries about the spectacular holiday time motorway crashes, most recently involving 100 vehicles, never failed to have graphic pictures. My favourite weather man, Paco, used excellent graphics and, unlike some of his colleagues, he mentioned the Canary Islands. I knew my Spanish was improving when I understood all that he said. A short 'interlude' film of surfing huge waves was mesmerising; the surfer not only ran the tube but also he played with it and occasionally popped over the far side of the breaking wave. I 'surfed' along with him, feeling his movements that were similar to power skiing.

Now I had a perfectly positioned base in a Canarian village.

Chapter 16
The Swallows

The first group of Swallows in the south of Tenerife was formed in 1985 when an advertisement in a bar in Los Cristianos attracted about twenty British residents. A founder member, Elaine Morgan, led the group for the first few years then Pearl took over; until her death in 2008 her sun never ceased to rise over the yardarm by 1100hrs at the Swallows' regular social coffee mornings. Here there is a much-appreciated book-swap arrangement and other weekly activities include painting (they hold an annual exhibition of their excellent work) line dancing, bowls and barbecues.

Many Swallows owning cars met to go on a walk at 1000hrs on Saturdays and Brian Hubbard, then the leader, organised where we'd stop for coffee en route to the start. I was pleased that their walks were in areas that were new to me, away from bus routes, and that the walks varied from week to week. Most were short, some at or near sea level, but others were in the foothills, 2-5000ft (600-1500m) with an uphill climb. Occasionally a walk had an impressive level of unperceived risk.

Depending on the length of the drive, often it was near noon before we left the cars and my first day with them was an example of the relaxed atmosphere of the group that rarely was fewer than twenty people. After an hour's gentle uphill stroll above Tijojo we stopped for picnic lunch. Robin immediately produced a 'bocadillo' (a bread roll filled with good things) and a flask of Ronmiel (a potent rum and honey mix). Afterwards the group went to a bar for a big meal, where Robin had a beer to quench his thirst, a gin and tonic appetiser and then a bottle of wine with the food. I enjoyed the company but, saddle-bagged with sweat, all I wanted was a bath and clean clothes, so at first I hung around until they'd finished lunch. When I knew them better I excused myself and found my own way back to base.

My first invitation to a party came from resident Swallow Vicky Aitkin, the kind physiotherapist who treated my severe back pain. After pre-dinner drinks at her house, we went to a restaurant, bought our meal and afterwards her husband, George, a gifted banjo player, provided excellent entertainment. Many Swallows were very talented and another resident, Elaine Morgan, generously volunteered her sewing skills to make a chair cover when I moved in to Adeje.

Non-resident Swallows, Barbara and Ken Ayling, were keen walkers and when I mentioned to them how sorry I was that our Swallows group never walked in the Cañadas – it was deemed too far to drive – in November 1994 they were the first brave walkers to join me for the easy two-hour walk around the García rocks. The weather was perfect, the rock colours and El Teide were posing for photographs and the only minus was being assaulted by the coaches' diesel fumes when we returned to the car park. The word must have gone around the Swallows, because later the group joined me on the near flat path to the tiny chapel at La Fortalezza near El Portillo. One day a small group walked with me to the spot where I'd photographed my crutches on my first visit. Ron Waterworth was the only Swallow to summit Guajara 8914ft (2717m) with me; his wife Mildred decided to stop at the ridge. Later, Welsh brothers Arwel and Nye wanted to do this more strenuous walk and again conditions were perfect; we met no one and the 342 bus gave us five hours for the average four-hour walk. The last section was on small, ball-bearing like stones. The altitude began to affect us, but we went slowly and had plenty of stops en route until we reached the summit for lunch and photographs. We'd seen only one couple all day and the panoramic views were a superb reward for our effort. But had I known that one brother had a heart condition I would have suggested a different walk.

Only Dafydd Johnson was unlucky enough to be with me on my only bad weather day at the Cañadas. Being used to mountains, his family has run the café on the A5 road near Ogwen Lake for fifty years. It was not luck that for a walk at 7,000ft above sea level he was well equipped with warm clothes and waterproofs. It was cloudy when we left the bus, raining by the time we reached the caves near the García rocks and it was dry just long enough for us to return to some shelter beside the Parador. This was closed for refurbishment and two very cold people ceased cowering on a window ledge and breathed a sign of relief on entering the warmth of the 342 bus.

When Ron and Ginny arrived they too were met by bad tempered clouds, but they didn't stop Ron, despite my protestations, from taking all the climbing gear to a small, wet crag. I had flu but, not wanting to miss an opportunity to climb an easy route near the Parador, I joined them when the sun returned. It was magical to be sitting on the top of the Cathedral rock that I had passed more times than I could remember when walking around the García rocks. I knew that rock here can be loose and friable and on the sloping summit it was very difficult to move a foot, or a rope, without sending down a shower of stones.

It was on their last day that we did the best walk I've done in Tenerife, along the rim of the Cañadas. The air temperature was freezing and the road was white with frost when we parked the car at the Parador and only when we reached the 'crutches' ridge did the sun feel really warm. Now we had to keep moving, because we had to catch the 342 bus before it left El Portillo at 1515hrs. The alternative was a long walk back or a very expensive taxi.

With unknown territory ahead my good military maps proved their worth. [1] The route was not clear, we met no one and lunch was but a pause, until at last El Portillo was below us but there was no obvious path - or time to look for one – because this last section of the walk was just off my map. We stayed on the wide track that we expected would lead to the main road below the Observatory. It did. From here it was about 2.5 miles (4kms) to El Portillo. We knew that one person might get a lift whereas three never would so I started to run-walk-run with the car keys. I got a lift with a park worker and was amused to be quizzed as to whether I was single and alone. The questioning ended as, with minutes to spare, he dropped me off by the 342. Ron and Ginny's week had started with serious Canarian winter weather but it had ended with a perfect day's walking above 7,000ft (2134m).

---

[1] These maps were available only from the military in Santa Cruz.

My most memorable day out with the Swallows, an ascent of a vegetation-filled, unused gully above Vilaflor, was very different. The two leaders, not Brian, said that they had walked the path. I doubted it. My landlady in Avenida Suecia had herded goats from Los Cristianos at sea level to the Cañadas and she remembered barrancos running with water throughout most of the winters. Traditional old paths were either near-horizontal, courting routes between villages that *crossed* barrancos or they went steeply uphill on *ridges*.

Only when our 'path' petered out did our leaders admit that they had not done the walk. Some of the group thought that they could find an easier route and they ended up on a steep bank while others were scattered all around. After some pulling, pushing and plenty of encouragement to surmount some irreversible moves up large boulders, eventually we found ourselves beside a water extraction factory a few metres from the road to El Teide. It was time for lunch and I was sure that now we would walk back down the road to Vilaflor.

I was wrong.

Up piped a penetrating female voice, "I don't like walking down a road."

Someone said that he knew another way down, so off we trooped *up* a track that joined the Teide road *up* which we walked for some time! Eventually we regrouped by a fire-prevention lookout tower (it is still there), before starting the descent. The leaders set off, soon to be out of sight, and were not seen again. As everyone scattered looking for a non-existent path, shouts and whistles resounded across the hillside. It was at this point that I ventured a suggestion. Once all were gathered in, minus the leaders, I went ahead to recce the easiest route. We kept contact with each other by looking *behind* us as well as ahead and one person became tail-end-Charlie. It was unknown territory but slowly, together, we eventually reached a building beside a large track that led to Vilaflor's football pitch and the road. Definitely we had a 'lorra, lorra luck' because on that 13th day in January 1996 no layer of cloud had rolled in at midday as often happens.

After a few years some Swallows had died and others like Brian had returned home to live in the UK. Bravely Tom and Barbara Young led the walkers for several years. To ensure that everyone heard where we'd meet at the start of the walk, Tom had a good idea. He blew a whistle to get everyone's attention. The result was his being called a dictator, behind his back. But during his leadership it was a rare Saturday when a chatterbox, who usually was too busy talking to listen, missed the walk. The risk of being sued, as the person who suggested the walk, or for anyone who led the group, was considerable; being strong is no qualification when unqualified and uninsured. Nowadays if anyone collapses or is in any trouble in the Cañadas, help comes with impressive speed. Only once did I ride accompanying someone in a Tenerife ambulance. Now younger members prefer long distance walks, some with knee crippling, steep descents. Sensibly, older members choose shorter routes rather than hold them back.

When someone fell on Guaza hill at the edge of Los Cristianos, it took many days and people looking before the search ended and the family were in mourning. I wanted to learn about rescues here and luckily Cristina's brother-in-law, Txema (José María Martín Rodriguez), worked with the emergency services. During one of his rest days I was delighted when he showed me round the centre that had been active since May 1998. 112 is the FREE number to phone in an emergency and it operates 24/7. It covered the whole archipelago, land

FREE

EMERGENCY

TELEPHONE NUMBER

1-1-2

It operates 24/7 and covers the whole archipelago, land and sea.
Interpreters receive calls in English, German, French, Italian & Spanish.

and sea and interpreters were available to receive calls in English, German, French, Italian and Spanish.

Four operators received calls directly onto their screen, they classified the information directly on their second screen and another operator had the job of listening and talking to any one of the four staff. This double checked and ensured the accuracy of the facts recorded. If very busy, a fifth operator could pass calls on to the 112 centre in La Palma, as happened when a storm hit Santa Cruz. Doctors were available to receive phone calls for advice 24 hours a day. Helicopters were based in El Hierro, La Palma, Gran Canaria and Tenerife and several were fully rescue equipped with a doctor available.

The centre in Santa Cruz was impressive, as was the intense concentration required by those who worked here. In six days, they worked for two mornings, two afternoons and two nights then had four days off; their rest breaks were taken when possible rather than dictated by the clock. I was lucky that the doctor on duty was not on the phone and had a few moments to talk to me.

With Canarian charm apologetically he said, "Usually it is Germans or British who walk alone, off paths, on malpais (badlands) and all too often they and their families pay the ultimate penalty for this error of judgement."

As if to confirm this I came across a lady with a twisted ankle. She was sitting on a park seat on the well used La Fortalezza path with a fabulous view of El Teide a mere 10 minutes' walk from the road. She was neither German nor British, she was Spanish.

Long spells of winter conditions in the Cañadas were becoming increasingly rare, but on one special day in the New Year, snow cover was perfect. With Barbara and Ken Ayling we drove to see El Teide wearing its smartest white winter duvet. The road had just been opened and with a very early start and empty roads our feet soon touched the roadside snow at the Cañadas. The scene was breathtakingly beautiful. Some plants had been transformed into snowballs and the aggressive approach of the lava flows was hidden beneath a sparkling blanket. We took photographs and only an occasional passing car and a piercingly loud solo performance of a bird nearby broke the peace.

Near the García rocks, the flat car park and any snow-covered slope had become a playground as gigantic plastic bags and other improvisations emerged from car boots. The atmosphere was intoxicating. With a backdrop of El Teide, what better sports arena could there be? In the warmth of the sun, we sat on the terrace of the Parador where the price of the coffee in this perfect setting was the same as most bars at the coast. Then a lady caught my eye, it was my hostess from the museum lunch. She advised us to start driving before the traffic became gridlocked.

The single, barely two-coach wide road across the Cañadas was narrowed further by snow and some very debonair parking. With cars arriving from both the north and the south there was a serious traffic flow problem. However, on this magical day no one was stressed, aggressive or unpleasant. While a vehicle was stationary, the sun, warmth and scenery appeared to have a drug-like, calming effect but the early birds had enjoyed the juiciest worm.

For some time now I'd seen and admired the courage of all those who decided to make their life in a foreign country about which they often knew so little, not least the language. Many young people as well as the retired come to Tenerife for the warm climate and the cheaper-than-the-UK cost of living, without central heating bills and with petrol being about half the price of the UK. Youngsters often did PR work, persuading passers-by to enter restaurants; one lost his job after boasting about his 8,000 pesetas (48 Euros) pay per night. A 'friend' volunteered to do his work for less money!

Those who did get residency were often retired couples who usually bought their apartment. Some young, single females have happy, successful marriages with local men as do older, divorced ladies. However, despite the many television programmes and warnings about the difficulties, a steady stream of couples, sometimes with more enthusiasm than research, sold their houses in the UK in order to start a bar or restaurant business. Rarely were they there for long. All too often the expat dream-bar in the sun faded and many returned home possibly wiser, usually poorer and all too often the blame would be firmly attributed to Tenerife. I met both couples and single foreigners who seemed to have kept their compass for life in their pocket while others had a self-confessed philosophy, 'it seemed a good idea at the time'. For them there was a steep learning curve.

I had a wonderful new experience, looking after a baby, when sadly the mother's partner went to prison in the north of the island. For her weekly one-hour visit, at 0900hrs, 1000hrs, 1100hrs or 1200hrs on a Sunday morning, she had an early start and a long and tedious bus journey from the south. If, as happened once, another visitor had been to see her partner at 0900hrs, then she'd a wasted journey. I was glad to help because life was difficult for her without his earnings and I enjoyed both looking after her lovely baby and even changing a nappy for the first time in my life. When I had to travel by bus the driver, my friend Martín, held the child on his lap while I folded the pram, opened the awkward, heavy, dirty, ground-level storage compartment door and put in the pram. [2] A childless life has many minuses and looking after the baby brought home to me how much I had missed.

By now I had a bank account to pay my monthly rental bills with the excellent Cajas De Ahorros Caja Canarias, where the staff were wonderfully helpful. Only one illogical aspect of the Spanish banking system never ceased to give me a wry smile. When I needed to transfer money from my deposit to my current account, they moved *all* the contents of my deposit account into my current account, left what money I needed in it and then returned the unwanted money back to a new page on the deposit account book.

Now, in addition to having made my will in the UK, I was advised to have a Spanish will drawn up and this was impressively straightforward. Then I learned more about life here. Some years after Pam Marchant had bought her cottage, we investigated the route to getting it registered; some time and much work was required on the property. Another challenge was when a friend, Peter, had problems with bank payments for his apartment. My Spanish was severely stretched when we met the non-English speaking lawyer in Santa Cruz. Thanks to the helpful staff in Grenadilla registry office, Pam knew what was required and Peter's bank problem file rose to the top of the huge pile on the lawyer's desk.

[2] The luggage compartment can be opened automatically by the driver on new buses.

Chapter 17
Village life

My apartment in Adeje had major pluses. As soon as I saw it I knew that its position in the village was perfect. It was spacious and, uniquely in this land of huge multi-apartment buildings, below me there were only four other families with whom to negotiate consideration regarding noise. On the ground floor, the owner of the apartments had an 'emporium'. This huge shop sold a multitude of items (an Englishman asked for - and got - a meat hammer) and it was closed only for the weekday siestas, Saturday afternoons and Sunday. When I had a flat-warming party I was delighted that with Cristina, her husband José and their young son Borja, Fernando, his wife Nell and their daughter, Neli. Since then I have been honoured to be invited to the homes of both families.

All my cooking and water heating was done by gas and this was essential for my nightly baths. My worry now was if it ran out on a Saturday afternoon the next delivery was not until Tuesday. Thanks to Alfredo, father of the owner, Javier Fraga, having a head-to-head discussion in my kitchen with an official from the Gas Company, with the paperwork in Javier's name I paid for the second gas bottle. I pitied the man who carried this heavy weight on his shoulder up seven flights of stairs; I could only move the full bottle by rolling it along its bottom rim (see page 147). The water and electricity were included in the rent and only if I used an enormous amount (unlikely) would I be charged for any surplus.

The first occupiers of houses in our road in Willaston were still calling families 'newcomers' twenty years after they had moved in, so I wasn't surprised that here a foreigner buying supplies daily in the street was looked upon with a certain amount of suspicion. I hoped that time would bring familiarity then friendship. There was no short cut, although I hoped that improving my language skills would help; meanwhile Canarian courtesy forgave my language inadequacies. I was sure that my every action was being watched, reported and discussed, not least because they knew an English girl who had arrived with a son and then had two more children with different fathers.

Javier's only comment was, "Working her way through the uniforms!"

I felt that the reputation of the British was on my shoulders. I must have been doing something right because gradually suspicious glances diminished, but it was a while before the next stage was reached. When I was seen, greetings were withheld until I'd made the first move, then I was rewarded with wonderful smiles.

My weekday routine started at 0800hrs when the local shop opened. The early birds bought anything from a few fresh bread rolls to an enormous basket full of ham and cheese, both sliced from a block, vegetables that had to be felt and fruit that was weighed. I knew that I was making progress when I received the greatest honour that a foreigner can be given – an old lady whose bag I'd carried from the shop to her front door offered me prior service knowing that I wanted only one bread roll.

My balcony overlooked the Plaza Cruz del Llano and prior to the nearby school gate being locked there was a solid traffic jam that extended back up the main street, the Calle Grande. Regularly drivers who had parked their car overnight in the Plaza would be blocked in and I had an entertaining ten minutes watching their body language when dealing with the culprit; their gestures would have impressed a race course bookie. While two local policemen were busy ensuring safety at the zebra crossing, cars were double-parked and general chaos reigned.

Very soon all was quiet and the bars had their first rush of the day as mothers and grandmothers chatted over a coffee. At 1000hrs construction workers had a short break; late evening meals ensured that having breakfast before leaving home wasn't a priority. From then on

Town Hall employees were seen in the cafes so about 0850hrs was the best time to catch them in their offices; they had arrived but usually they would not have gone into a meeting or elsewhere. By 1100hrs there was a wave of visitors arriving, a few early walkers were returning from the Barranco del Infierno and retired men were sitting chatting on pavement seats. At 1400hrs both the building and the street were quiet. The only movement was the occasional patter of walkers' booted feet until, on weekdays, at 1700hrs the street came alive again.

At 1800hrs some bars in the Calle Grande filled with beer-drinking construction workers talking loudly over the football commentary on TV, a very male-oriented time that once was 'taken over'. A group of middle-aged Liverpudlian ladies, still wearing beach clothing, mainly short shorts and sun tops, replaced the football by music, dancing and singing. The spectator numbers swelled as the construction workers were squeezed out to join the pop-eyed old men on the pavement. This session, which lasted until the group departed for a meal, was long remembered as was the only robbery in the street when a woman had her handbag snatched. By closing, at 2000hrs, the shops were at their busiest - there was a definite tendency to do things at the last minute if not later! From 2100hrs there was chatter and clatter during the preparation and eating of evening meals in the apartments below me.

Saturday was different; the street's vibrancy gathered pace throughout the morning, reaching its peak before some shops and bars closed for the weekend. From 1400hrs until Monday morning all was very quiet. However, restaurants famous for Canarian spicy chicken stayed open during the weekend and had their one day of rest in the week. Situated at the highest point of the village beside the entrance to the Barranco del Infierno was one of the largest restaurants. This family business had many tables both inside and on a terrace, great views and even some car parking space. All restaurants had their faithful, regular customers and I recommend that visitors make their own decision by the fairest method, the 'Egon Ronay' tests.

There was more to Adeje than bars and restaurants. The attractive sixteenth-century church, Santa Úrsula, and the plaza beside it were the centre of religious activities. While the Casa Fuerte, situated by the cannon a little below the famous Barranco del Infierno walk, had been built in the 1550s to defend locals from pirates, Arabs and English, including Sir Francis Drake who ransacked it in 1589. Sadly, the building was destroyed by fire in 1902 and, although it was declared a historic monument in 1986, it still is not open to the public.

In winter, when locals considered 20°C cold, their windows were shut and usually it was possible to get to sleep by 2300hrs. Summer, however, was different. With windows open, voices penetrated and smokers, leaning out of their rooms, talked loudly to those in their apartment or to their neighbours a few feet away. When the Spanish holiday month of August brought freedom from work routine and many visiting relatives, my severely disturbed sleep had the usual result; some nights neither calamine nor cool cream calmed my torture. I'd sit in bed frustrated by the need to sleep, crying and scratching at the same time. But I had escaped from the UK pollen and the need for steroids in my eyes, nose, lungs and even systemically.

Being level with the Sahara where temperatures in summer have reached 58°C, it was no surprise that I found it difficult to do anything because soon after sunrise the sun's power was too much for me. But I'd not done the famous local walk, the Barranco del Infierno. [1] It started at the highest point of the village about 1,000ft (300m) rising only 1148ft (350m) in its 2 mile (3.2km) length. So, early one morning, I set off along this easy, short, linear route. The start was typical south Tenerife, dry and arid but suddenly at about half way the conditions changed. The vegetation increased, the ground underfoot became damp and I realised that in winter the little footbridges over dry mud patches or a tiny stream would be needed. Beside the pool below the dripping remains of the waterfall, there were a few people but I didn't stay long; the peace was superb and I met no one on the walk.

Protection from the sun was vital and I went everywhere in a long skirt with my blouse sleeves rolled down, a decent hat and my hands in the skirt pockets. I'd seen an old lady who was sure that the skin cancer on the back of her hands was due to a lifetime of horse riding without wearing gloves. But sweating was impossible to avoid because many walks, even those in shade, were without a breeze.

The Swallows started walking at midday, 'mad dogs and

---

[1] Entry is now controlled. It is best to book the walk, phone: 922 782885.

Englishmen', or occasionally at 1700hrs in the accumulated heat of the day. So I was delighted when Ron Waterworth agreed to start early from Adeje and walk to Taucho. The sun was below El Conde as we walked up the Calle Grande and immediately a small Canarian dog joined us. Much as we tried to send it away it wouldn't go and soon it was enjoying the multitude of opportunities to send lizards scurrying for shelter under bushes.

With the sun above El Conde the heat increased and Ron decided that the dog needed a drink; he converted a plastic bag into a water bowl. My worry was what we'd do with the dog when we met a friend in Taucho. Luckily he was still driving an old Citroën so he had no objections to the dog being put on the floor underneath Ron's feet; we said our goodbyes where the dog had found us, in the Calle Grande.

To sit on the shady side of the street at a bar's outside table and try to read the newspaper that was always available improved my Spanish and the excellent coffee cost less than the paper. In it I saw an invitation to join a guided walk in the San Lorenzo Valley some distance away starting at 0900hrs so I rang to book a place. I knew that I'd have to take a taxi but a shock awaited me. No one was there.

I was getting seriously worried when, exactly on time, a kind man came to tell me that the walk was cancelled due to insufficient numbers. I could have hugged him. I showed him my military maps, he pointed out the route and I headed off towards a narrow cleft in a hillside above. The path was obvious and on it I met a man descending, leading a donkey with two large oil barrels strapped to its side. He confirmed my destination and in clear Spanish he explained that he'd been maintaining machinery in the water pumping station that was hidden in a cleft in the hill. This became known among the Swallows as the 'Donkey Walk'.

Corpus Christi, an important date in the Canarian calendar, was not in my diary so seeing all the preparations for this special day in June for the first time was a real surprise. In the north of Tenerife there were magnificent floral street carpets, but in the drier south Adeje locals made theirs from dyed salt. To ensure that no two carpets were the same, the co-ordinator received all the plans; their complexity depended upon the experience of the makers. Among the many regular contributors were the local police, the firemen, the hotel Bahia del

Plans for the Corpus Christi carpet

Duque and the Casa de Mayores (the retired centre). All the materials were provided by the Town Hall.

Work started around midday on Saturday when the Calle Grande and a parallel street, Calle Corpus Christi, were closed. Then they were swept and washed prior to measuring-poles being used to mark the edge of the carpet and the names of those responsible for each section written in chalk. The work started early in the evening and later extra lights were run out from nearby houses; some people were still carefully spreading the grains with a spatula well after midnight had come and gone. Cleverly, members of the Casa de Mayores saved their knees by making their carpet with paper resting on a table. Throughout the day the carpet lay in state to be admired and photographed; neither dog nor vandal had dared to walk upon it. After the Sunday evening church service the religious procession passed through the streets demolishing all the beautiful handiwork - and before dawn next day the street was clean!

Finding something to do in the three summer months was helped when Adeje's University Summer School advertised a one-week course in July on 'Conflict between the Environment and Tourism'. I enrolled. I doubted that I'd understand much but it was worth a try and hopefully the cost. However by the time the classes started at 1600hrs the classrooms had accumulated an unbearable level of heat and the air conditioning was too noisy to be used. Added to this I found it too hot to cook a proper meal before 1600hrs and I was too tired afterwards to be bothered to eat much. I needed the month of September to recover after these summers.

Most students were undergraduates from La Leguna University and their attendance for a week was compulsory; they accumulated points that would count towards their final degree. Sadly some interesting topics were ruined by some dreadful presentation; with elbows on the table some lecturers read sheet after sheet of typed script non-stop for 30-40 minutes. This efficiently demolished any interest the class might have had and my ability to concentrate. Long-winded questions seemed to be designed primarily to show off the questioner's knowledge and usually answers were of an interminable length – making the course too much for me!

My survival was thanks to Estafanía Hernandez Fariña. This charming, intelligent lady worked in a bank in Las Américas and although much younger than me she had a similar sense of humour. I had listed the teaching errors and realised, too late, that she had read and understood them. We had a laugh and thanks to her ability to understand my Spanish we chatted and I survived the week. I was glad that I did! On the last day a tall, Germanic-looking man speaking excellent Castillian Spanish used the overhead projector correctly by revealing information topic by topic.

His first statement made everyone sit up, "This island has plans, mountains of plans, but actions, none."

The class sat riveted as he outlined problems that needed to be solved; his excellent talk had covered everything that could be said and significantly not one question was asked afterwards!

The week ended with a visit to La Gomera; however, even Estafanía's best efforts failed to find any information about the day ahead, so I went with plenty of survival food. It was not until after the lunch at 1500hrs that we learned that the meal *was* included in the cost of the excursion. We were even promised a booklet of all the lectures, but, again despite Estafanía's many phone calls and even her personal visit to a well-hidden office in La Leguna, it didn't appear; a year later we deemed it a lost cause! The whole course had been something of an endurance test but my great fortune was that I had found a loyal friend. Despite her moving to work nearer to her parents in Arafo, I've enjoyed her excellent company ever since.

From my first visit I'd taken photographs everywhere I went. My little Rollei 35 camera did its best and at Photo Teide I was impressed by the efficiency and consistently high printing standard. This family business took official photographs of village activities such as first communions. Later I discovered two other family businesses well hidden in side streets.

In 1935 the father of Pedro, the present owner, had left their family mill in Arona (it closed in 1970), to come to Adeje, to marry and to open a mill here. Pedro, 72 years old, or his son, Manuel, ordered the wheat from Santa Cruz and the delivery lorry almost breathed in as it entered the tiny side street. It held its breath while a metal corkscrew within the feeding tube drew 10,000 kilos of grain upwards into the mill's hopper, still the original, sturdy, easy to maintain machine.

After filtering and cleaning by air, no chemicals or additives here, they produced their three-cereal pack - 50% wheat and 25% each of maize and barley - and the popular gofio made by toasting wheat that passes through temperatures up to 400°C. Nearby a family-run bread shop was above the bakery. Here seven mornings a week, 0800-1400hrs, the wonderful Virginia Gonzalez Guirola chatted with Manolo Pérez Bello and other customers; with eyes as bright as a chaffinch, this tiny of stature but large in intelligence, delightful character was many years older than Pedro!

I was hanging out my washing on my rooftop (azotea), when the noise of a helicopter attracted my attention. The washing could wait and I rushed off to find out what was happening. New pipes were being lifted up to the old concrete watercourse that ran horizontally across the hillside near Adeje. Pilot Carlos from Helicópteros Insulares SL explained that the pipes would bring water from galleries in Fasnia, miles away, to slake the thirst of the fast-growing Costa del Adeje at a rate of 40 litres per second. He had trained in America where flying was

Ostrich farm

cheaper but no one wanted to employ an inexperienced pilot. With great courage and initiative he hired a helicopter in winter from mainland Spain when charges were at their lowest and then gained experience wherever he could, including hunting for tuna in Madagascar. Now Carlos had invested in this Allouette helicopter that can carry 750 kilos or up to seven people for 175,000 pesetas, about 1000 Euros (£690) per hour.

By now I knew more local people and it was thanks to Teresa in Arona's tourist office that I heard that the first ostrich farm in the Canary Islands was opening on Friday 20th August 1999. It was conveniently positioned two kilometres above the autopista exit to Tenerife South Airport. My admiration for the initiative of the owner, Juan Vicens, knew no bounds. Ostriches can live for seventy years, be fertile for around 30 years and survive temperature variations as great as –10°C to 50°C. Each of the 14 pens contained one male - whose vigour dictates the numbers of his female companions! After 42 days the delicate hatchlings spent 7 weeks in pens with an overnight temperature of 25°C and then in the large pens before going to the Matadero, abattoir, in La Leguna. Then they returned to Juan who de-boned and packed the meat for distribution to restaurants and supermarkets.

In his restaurant, open 1100-2300hrs, a one-egg omelette could feed eight people while the healthy red meat, low in fat cholesterol, was cooked for a very short time on low heat; longer made it tough and frying was not advised due to rapid water evaporation. This enterprising man also sold egg shells (they became lamp shades), feathers and skins. For some time the local Town Hall allowed kennels for 30 stray dogs to be installed next door to the farm and their barking resulted in a 50% drop in egg production. However, despite being dogged by problems, relief came when eventually the Town Hall realised that a quality business was good publicity. In 2005 visits by local school children began with the warning that ostriches had very strong feet and a long reach; they were addicted to glasses so you had to keep out of pecking range. Visitors could even be photographed sitting on a – tightly controlled – ostrich and if they bought meat, their nominal entrance fee was refunded.

One of many advantages of staying in Adeje was that the bus stop was by my front door. I surprised myself that I enjoyed the special tone of the engine as it pulled the long, double bus from my plaza into the Calle Grande. An example of the small, family atmosphere of TITSA was the timetable of the 111 bus. It started its journeys at the Hotel Abinque, Torviscas, *except* at 0530hrs when it started at Adeje then it went via the Abinque twice to Santa Cruz before returning to Adeje at 1315hrs. Here another driver took over, did the same and finally returned at 2115hrs to Adeje where the bus was parked overnight. In my innocence I thought that this direct service to Santa Cruz was for the convenience of Adejeños, but when Adeje driver, Renaldo, retired this service stopped! I'd seen Renaldo look in his rear view mirror, see youngsters at the back misbehaving and as he walked, slowly, towards them they visibly shrank. I never expected to be sitting near to Renaldo while learning to play the guitar or see him playing an important role in La Pasión at Easter.

I felt as though I'd lost a friend when I heard that the buses were to be re-routed away from the Calle Grande to some way below my plaza. I was determined to have a photograph of the double bus negotiating the extremely sharp, 90° turn to enter and descend the

Calle Grande. On the last day I was at this corner trying out different positions before the bus arrived when a local policeman approached, smiling and curious. Fidel was different; this kind man had a beard and was taller than most of his colleagues. He offered to stop the bus for me and this he did, several times, so that I had a choice of photographs. A long time later I was amazed that he remembered me; he crossed the street and to the surprise of all around us he gave me a kiss on each cheek. This charming man was a friend of Teresa, who sat beside me in Guicho's music class, and her husband, Juan José was also a local policeman.

I'd been renting the apartment for several years when a family friend, Brian Griffiths, came to visit and during his stay he rented a car. The freedom and convenience of visiting lots of places in one day, to leave whenever we felt like it and not least to control the temperature in the car, convinced me that it was time to stop thinking about it and to buy a car. After much research, four months later, in June 1999, I did just that and thereby more doors opened.

Chapter 18
Car owner

Thanks to travelling on the buses I'd met many local people, but only after I'd moved to Adeje and was in need of company did I travel regularly at 2100hrs for the short journey to Stephan's bar in Las Américas with driver Andrés. A middle aged lady was usually on the bus when I entered and once, when he was early, Andrés stopped at the petrol station between Adeje and Torviscas and returned with sweets for us.

While he was away I asked the lady, "Are you going to work?"

"Yes," she said.

"Where do you work?"

"On the street, you've got to work somewhere," was her reply.

I respected her pragmatic outlook on life.

Some time later I was returning to Adeje at midday on a very crowded bus when, still dressed for work, the lady saw me, waved and then sat beside me. As we chatted there were looks of incredulity on the faces of the driver and the visitors around us! Bus travel had become rather like sharing a large car with friends. When buses were re-routed for road works, the driver did not see me at the temporary bus stop but Apolonia from Guía de Isora spotted me. She told the driver to stop and he did! Later I was glad to return Andrés' kindness by bringing from the UK a Roberts radio that he'd asked me to buy.

But too many days seemed to be wasted with basic shopping trips. There were about twenty bus stops, the number changed as the routes were altered; between Adeje and Los Cristianos the journey could take an hour. Brian had shown me that by avoiding shift-change times I could drive to Los Cristianos in 10 minutes. For advice about what to buy, I went to Bill Foster, my first landlord, who had run a car hire business.

His immediate response was, "Look for anything Japanese."

Most small, secondhand cars for sale in the south were Clios and I was glad that a friend, who had lived in Santa Cruz and knew his way around, had offered to take me. He loved driving and my only concern was that his risk thermometer exceeded the 120kph speed limit. Usually his left hand was on the steering wheel while the other was thrust through the spokes, his fingers tapping upon the dashboard. Added to this was an unstoppable torrent of words on whatever topic he had on his mind.

At our first stop, there on the garage forecourt was a Nissan Micra 1000cc, two years old. If all else was equal I believed that a car's bright colour (the RAF air sea rescue helicopters are yellow) could aid collision avoidance. This car was a vivid red, it had my initials before marriage, BL, and it was love at first sight. With Mapfre's provisional insurance and a cheque, next day the car was mine.

Despite the queue of cars following a hire car driver who braked sharply just before and accelerated after every bend, Arcadio's passengers always had a smooth ride. The following morning I made an early start to 'christen' my car with a drive to the Parador; it was fun to drive up this familiar road when it was deserted. Now I needed to leave permanently in the car a red triangle (later two were needed), spare light bulbs and a pair of my spectacles. To these I added a metallic sun reflector, a sponge and plenty of rags to dry the car, otherwise the high calcium levels in the water left unsightly streaks and spots.

Six weeks later, when the final paperwork still had not come from the police, I rang the salesman.

He said what he should have said at the beginning, "To buy a car you need a Número de Identificación de Extranjeros (an identification number for foreigners)."

To obtain the NIE required visits to the police station, patience while standing in the long queues, and a wait of at least 40 days before my NIE certificate arrived. Armed with my insurance, other documents and their photocopies, I went to find Tráffico in Santa Cruz.

Here I joined the queues, first for a numbered ticket, then to pay 1,000 pesetas (6 Euros) per document and finally to receive the stamped, authorised *copies* of my documents. At least everything was in the same building!

Before the offices closed for lunch I even had time to pop next door to learn about the driving test. Here the computer screen had two unsynchronised, waving lines moving upwards and each line had a cursor that should be kept within the narrow space. It was harder than I expected.

Curious I asked, "How many drivers fail this test?"

Smiling, the lady replied, "None, because they've had to pass a doctor's physical examination before coming here."

Whether in a car or on foot it is advisable always to carry with you a photocopy of your passport, your European Health Insurance Card and private health insurance, because if injured often the ambulance staff ask whether you have these details. Even if you have private health insurance you can go to the Green Clinic, the very busy national health hospital in Las Américas; but if you choose to enter, and not to use your private insurance, and the Green Clinic hospital has no beds available for you, then you could be taken to a hospital in Santa Cruz fifty miles away!

All this paperwork saved me from increasing the police coffers because drivers could be stopped at any time; without the paperwork I'd be given an immediate fine. Now the original documents were safe in my apartment and the copies stayed in my handbag; if left in the car they'd be a gift to a thief. Unfortunately, thieves look for careless visitors. I was on a cliff top near Santa Cruz looking down at the Playa de Las Teresitas beach, when I turned and saw two young men of middle-eastern appearance a few metres away. Through binoculars they were looking down at people 'hiding' their precious items in their car boot before they went to sunbathe. Parking at the side of a busy main road prior to going for a long walk en route to or in El Teide National Park risked returning to a smashed window; some people now leave their empty car unlocked.

Sadly, thieves also operated in supermarkets. A skilled '5-fingered shopper' had stolen a friend's purse from her *front*-positioned, supposedly safe waist belt - and cheekily they'd closed the zip! For more information I requested and got an informative tour with the manager of Mercadona in Las Américas. Here I was horrified to see the number of easy pickings that were available in customer's open-mouthed handbags and fashion mini-rucksacks. Now I understood why he said that they dealt daily with a genuine loss as well as with some clients who tried to walk out with free groceries - by falsely reporting a stolen purse!

It wasn't easy to find a parking space in a small (safer) garage. At first the wonderful Mário, owner of the excellent Mário's bar in San Lorenzo, gave me free parking below his unfinished house. With a rough stone floor, builder's materials all around and only my headlight illumination, avoiding the concrete pillars made parking a challenge. Later it stayed in a garage in Costa del Adeje but the cost monthly was outrageous; it was the same as the rent for my apartment. It was a relief when a space beside José and Cristina's car became available in Adeje for 49 Euros (£34) a month; it was five minutes' walk.

To reduce the risk of condensation at the end of a day's flying, the plane's tanks were always left full of fuel, so before my return to the UK I did the same with my car. With volcanic dust everywhere, after covering the car with an old curtain, on top of it went a cheap, large, thin plastic sheet bought in Trujillo builder's merchant nearby.

With European money pouring into the island, at the end of the 1990s came the major road-widening scheme on the main road below Adeje. It was here that it happened. In the slow moving, long queue of cars, my view ahead was blocked by a huge 4x4 when unexpectedly my passenger reached across and moved my sun visor. My attention was distracted, the traffic stopped, the car didn't and very discreetly my little Nissan went into the back of the nearest thing to a tank that is driven on tarmac; Arcadio drove past while I was examining my crumpled bonnet. Now all the bus drivers would know. At the Mapfre car insurance office the wonderfully helpful Juan García Martín inspected my car and Alfredo, Javier's father, told me where it could be repaired. Three days later I was driving again but the following year my premium was increased, thereby inflating a comprehensive insurance that already was three times higher than in the UK!

It was a different story four years later when, tired, instead of putting my car in the garage I'd left it in the Plaza. Paco lived immediately above where I'd parked and he heard the crunch; a car had been shunted by the one behind into the back of mine. Paco spoke to the drivers and during their chat he told them that I was in the same night school class as his wife. A paper with both drivers' details was still on my windscreen when I returned to the car next morning! Despite Juan's best efforts with the complications of two drivers' companies involved, this time authorisation for the repair took much longer. The village garage that serviced my car did the work while I was in the UK and Cristina's husband, José, regularly checked the progress. The rear windscreen wiper wasn't working when I returned: it was soon fixed – but having to re-fill the empty tank was a surprise!

The annual car tax paid to the town hall ran from 1st January to 31st December and the payment, about 45 Euros (£31) had to be made within a designated two months, but the months chosen varied from year to year. The very impressive, Government-run ITV (MOT) pronounced ee-tay-oovay was renewed on the car's birthday. After presenting the paperwork in the office, I joined one of the two lines of cars moving slowly into a shed high enough to receive the tallest vehicle.

First to be checked were the seat belts, indicators and brake lights. From then on, factory-like, we progressed through the shed as lights and exhaust, wheels and brakes were tested. Finally, I carefully drove the car above an inspection pit. The front wheels rested on metal pads that moved sideways, testing the suspension and a man in the pit beneath me spoke into a microphone telling me in Spanish when to jiggle the steering wheel in different directions. All was computerised, very clean (the staff wore immaculate, grease-free grey outfits) and very, very efficient. I needed two new tyres and, to their surprise, although I had about two weeks' grace, within an hour I was back through the shed and a new ITV sticker was put on the windscreen.

The ITV was one of the rare occasions when I saw locals waiting with worried expressions and doubts about the outcome. The inspection dates became more frequent as the car aged and two years later I'd forgotten the ITV; I was lucky not to have been stopped and fined by the police. Panicking at 0700hrs next day, I found all was quiet, only one line was operating, the testers chatted, posed for photographs and my car passed the inspection.

ITV inspection
A superbly run, efficient MOT system.

In Adeje village overnight, some parking rules, such as leaving a car on a zebra crossing, were overlooked. But when notices appeared warning drivers *not* to park between certain hours on a day stated then signs should be obeyed. At 2000hrs local police and men wearing overalls and lumiglow jackets surrounded the three lonely vehicles left in the Plaza: señalisación (road sign repainting) was about to begin. Two owners came running to remove their cars, the third managed to persuade the driver of the grua (tow away truck) to off-load his 4x4. Then started a couple of hours of mesmerising efficiency as some markings were noisily ground away before the spaces between movable metal strips were sprayed with white paint.

Only once did I return to find a parking ticket on my windscreen. I'd driven (the early bird got the best vegetables) to a delightful local market. Here I bought supplies both for myself and for Alison's parents, Doris and Bryan Cox, who wintered in Pueblo Torviscas. I was delighted and surprised that I found a parking place near their apartment for the few minutes it would take me to deliver the goods. But they didn't always hear my knock on the door that was always double locked. On my return the ticket was on the windscreen and I'd just missed the traffic warden.

I was in the appropriate office in Adeje's Town Hall fifteen minutes later. By now I was learning the Canarian approach to problems. In my improving but far-from-perfect Spanish I told a charming lady my long, convoluted story about wonderful local produce, an old couple who needed help and so on. I was concentrating hard on thinking in Spanish and I barely noticed a man standing nearby. When finally I'd finished, he stepped forward saying that he was the Town Hall's lawyer. He took the ticket, photocopied it and smiling said that fines for parking there were not legal and that I'd hear no more. I didn't. And when I was told that the chip on my windscreen would be repaired in an hour an a half, with the nicest smile I could muster, I asked gently whether it was an English or Canarian hour and a half. A pause, realisation and big smile later the reply was English. It was. (See p.178/9, Complaint to a Town Hall.)

The car gave me the freedom to meet Estafanía at attractive villages on the coast that were half way between her home in Arafo and Adeje and to visit places such as delightful Vilaflor whose bus service was infrequent. I loved this unspoilt village where, despite the attractions of work in tourism, rural life was valued and respected. It was not unusual to see men with backs bowed under their loads of animal fodder and I was glad that Frank Wisby had introduced me to Daniela who lived here.

Every time we met, this interesting lady gave me a wonderful welcome and from her I learned more about the Canarian way of life. Fascinated I watched her make rosquetes, a Canarian Christmas delight. The dough was made from a huge amount of flour, 15 eggs, a bowl of milk and one of olive oil and some aniseed. After rolling a 12cm (five inch) long sausage, she curled it into a circle and put it on a clean table cloth. When the table was full each one was fried in a pan of oil then dipped into sugar melted in a little water.

In August 1999, Tenerife had a 25% maximum eclipse of the moon and, as we drank her herbal drink, made from plants in her garden, Daniela told me about an eclipse in October 1959. She was picking grapes with her father and sister when it began. They had no warning;

the dogs became nervous, the birds were confused and their donkey began to yawn.

At the coast, with new roads came the fastest sprouting of hotels and complexes that I'd ever seen and all too soon Adeje itself was expanding. Where I nearly bought an apartment came huge residential blocks where workers could buy two and three bedroom apartments at reduced prices. (The earlier phase of social housing had been small, single storey bungalow style houses.) Inevitably the need for both water and electricity, a thirst more voracious than for any crop, had arrived. Fans and air conditioning outnumbered both solar panels and environmentally kind construction, all amidst promises of environmental protection. 'Quality tourism' was the cry as water was poured onto a desiccated landscape to create golf courses, incongruous splashes of green!

It was thanks again to Teresa, a wonderfully helpful lady in Arona's Tourist Office in Las Américas, that I heard about the well-hidden Institute of Technology and Renewable Energy. It was founded by the Tenerife Government in December 1990, a few kilometres north of San Isidro, and windmills guided me to the unsigned autopista exit. The park had solar panels, an original wind turbine, photovoltaic and other environmentally friendly sources of energy. Even in August and without air conditioning, the building was refreshingly cool inside because its walls were built of 'marmol trevertino', a porous material. Just below the roof there were air vents and on the windward side of the building both the small pool and the grass around it were maintained by desalinated water, whose evaporation assisted in the cooling of the building. Groups from schools and colleges were being shown everything that can be done to save the environment; meanwhile construction work continued as usual.

I returned to this interesting place several years later to see the expensive wooden houses, raised a little above the ground to allow cool air to enter from below; it left through vents in the ceiling. Admiring them at the same time was an architect, Victor, his wife, daughter and mother, Hortensia, with whom I chatted and exchanged addresses. This dynamic lady has become a valued friend; we meet regularly and she has stayed with me in Bangor. But the houses were built with wood imported from Canada.

REGISTRO DE ENTRADA

*Por favor utilice letras mayúsculas y rellene cada casilla con una sola letra.

NOMBRE:																		
PRIMER APELLIDO:																		
SEGUNDO APELLIDO																		
D.N.I./T.R.NUM.:																		
TELEFONO:																		
DOMICILIO:																		

La persona cuyos datos identificativos quedan expresados,

EXPONE:

EN SU VIRTUD,

Solicita , que teniendo por admitido este escrito y prévios los trámites que juzgue pertinentes se digne resolver como en el mismo se pide.

VILLA DE ADEJE, A DE DE 2002.

SR. ALCALDE-PRESIDENTE DEL ILUSTRE AYUNTAMIENTO DE LA VILLA DE ADEJE
C / GRANDE,1- 38670 - Adeje Tel. 922-75-62--00- Fax 922-71-04-05

The Adeje Town Hall (Ayuntamiento) form for making a complaint

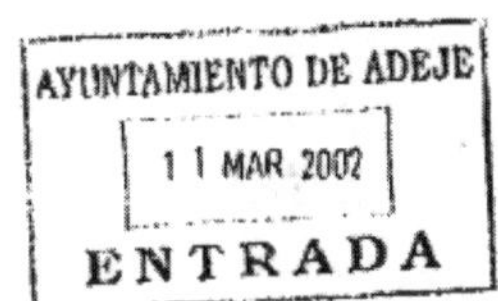

REGISTRO DE ENTRADA

*Por favor utilice letras mayúsculas y rellene cada casilla con una sola letra

NOMBRE:	B A R B A R A J A N E
PRIMER APELLIDO:	J A M E S
SEGUNDO APELLIDO	NO HAY
D.N.I./T.R.NUM.:	X 0 2 8 6 0 4 6 5 - R
TELEFONO:	9 2 2 7 1 0 7 3 5
DOMICILIO:	E D I F. P A A G A A No 2, A D E J E

La persona cuyos datos identificativos quedan expresados,

EXPONE:

OBRAS en la carretera

GUIA de Isora

MIRAVERDE

Aqui hay un agojero grande que molesta ~~mi~~ mi coche pequeña mucho.

Las Américas

Por favor, llena este agojero –temporalamente o lo que puede usted – al nivel del tarmac de la carretera

VILLA DE ... 11 de MARZO DE 2002

[signature] James

A completed form

My complaint was about a large hole in the road.
The repair was made with impressive speed.

I was told that it was more expensive to produce electricity in Tenerife than in mainland Spain and UNELCO, the company that then had the monopoly on the island, was believed to be receiving a grant for every unit of electricity that it sold. Perhaps this was why there was a dearth of solar panels? In Greece I'd seen no building, however modest, without one. To fulfil people's obsession for a view, climbing up every hill that faced the sea were apartments, their mandatory huge plate glass windows protected from summer's African-strength sun by enormous blinds outside and with reflective curtains and fans inside. That suddenly electricity was urgently required was a surprise? The next thing I heard was that putting high voltage cables through the last area of unspoilt countryside in the south including Vilaflor was deemed the only solution.

Members of the Green Party (Los Verdes de Canarias), local residents (La Plataforma Cuidana) Daniela and many others from Vilaflor and nearby villages gathered in San Isidro's plaza. I was very impressed by an attractive, well groomed lady who spoke so clearly that I could understand most of her words. When she came down from the

Señalisación, re-painting road markings

In Adeje this very well organised work usually started in the evening.

stage I spoke to her and immediately Eulalia Espinosa Dorta asked if I would speak too. As foreigners were the main source of the island's income and 'quality' tourism was being trumpeted in local papers, I thought 'why not?'. Despite my many errors, they understood when I said that not everyone came to Tenerife to rest, relax or to get drunk. It was the Canarian people, their beautiful countryside and peaceful walks that had guaranteed my return.

At first an example of the headline in Spanish and English newspapers (I was writing regularly for the *Tenerife News*) was 'Pylons no, Pines yes'. I emphasised that this project would bring shame to the whole island, not just to Vilaflor. Under the guidance of tiny Vilaflor's hard working, school teacher mayor, José Luis Fumero, the campaign grew until, in 2002, came the 'grand manifestacion', the big protest march; 100,000 people filled the streets of Santa Cruz. There was massive press and TV coverage and this time, to a TV camera, I did my best to voice the horror of many foreigners at the prospect of the planned pylons. Impressed by the strength of this campaign the government promised that an alternative method would be found. Recently the pylons were installed alongside the autopista.

However, risks to the environment in the south have never ceased. A large, new, commercial port is spreading like cancer along the coast below Grenadilla. It is beside the Institute of Renewable Energy, upwind of, and near to the popular beaches in the south. Olivia Stone wrote in 1889, 'I wish I had a pen of fire with which to beg, beseech, command, threaten or do anything that would make the authorities really prevent the wholesale destruction of trees that takes place'.[1]

In 2003 Vilaflor Town Hall won my heartfelt admiration. A superb professional music teacher, María Angeles Cabrera Siverio, trained a mostly retired group, including Daniela, to reach concert standard, singing 'Ave María' in parts. So it was a shock when, in 2006, Vilaflor started to build more 'casa rurales' rural houses. They bore no resemblance to the old, small, attractive, discreetly tucked away single story Canarian buildings. Incongruous two storey houses now march up a skyline a few kilometres below Vilaflor. Did we save Vilaflor from pylons so that, after José Luis Fumero's retirement from being Mayor, these buildings could be peppered around the village?

---

[1] *Tenerife and its six satellites*, by Olivia Stone. Marcus Ward. 1889.

Campaigns always increase publicity for a cause and I read in the Spanish papers about two more. In January 2002, hunters gathered at Chio, Boca Tauche and at El Portillo, three entrances to El Teide National Park; they wanted to protect their right to hunt muflones (a type of goat) and rabbits. Hunting continues, starting at the end of August and ending about two months later, with the number of dogs limited and other restrictions.

The belt of protection in the park had been tightening yearly. At first I'd seen 10-strong groups of men frantically wielding Dutch-spade type instruments, clearing the paths of stones and marking the edges with larger stones to make a wide rural pavement. Restrictions to visitor access to the summit of El Teide and to the caves near the García rocks followed, and now a big mechanical digger widens a track. Recently, unwanted roadside parking has been prevented by grotesque barriers; banks of volcanic debris would have blended better in this magnificent scenery. In my first visit, Juanma, a park guide, told me about the plan to keep cars outside the park and to charge for rides in the Park transport inside. This has not happened yet and with luck it won't in my time.

The other campaign involved groups of coach drivers. With placards they were standing at the side of a minor road just above Tenerife South Airport. I was horrified to learn that if they worked an 8-hour day, 5 days a week, they were paid only 493 Euros (£340) a month. For a better wage they did longer hours than might be allowed elsewhere and they had no tachograph because the distances driven were too small to be valid. If they had an accident, they told me, they personally were blamed, not the company for whom they worked. Despite the fact that TITSA drivers drove greater distances during their 8-hour shift, coach drivers envied them their better work conditions and stronger safety rules. Those working for TITSA often used the remainder of the day for other employment.

Chapter 19
Life with Adejeños

Much as the car had freed me from time wasted waiting at bus stops, so being in Adeje gradually released me from long summers and evenings alone. I began to meet and socialise with local people around me.

Living in the apartment below was Beatrice Castro, a single mother, who invited me to join her for Noche Buena, 24th December 1997. Like our Christmas Day it was a time for family gatherings and I met her son, Omar, partner and Grandpa, Gregorio, from La Palma, whom she called father. Their generosity, food, wine and friendship overcame my lack of fluency in their language. I knew Canarian men who lived here with foreign partners but I'd met no Canarian lady who'd gone to live abroad. At eighteen Bea had met and married a German, she'd lived in his country for ten years and when the marriage ended she'd returned alone to work in Tenerife.

Despite our age difference we were similar in many ways. Not only did she suffer from eczema but also for several years she had – as I did when training Infantry soldiers - an unusual job for a woman. She'd translated some very unpleasant topics when working for the Guardia Civíl Police. Later, her intelligence, drive, initiative and persistence enabled her to progress through the daunting paperwork required to open a health shop in Costa del Adeje in 2003. It is doing well. And, in March 2008, I was honoured when she took me to the attractive Aridane valley, La Palma, to meet her family at Gregorio's 90th birthday party.

Only once have I been 'picked up' in Adeje high street and this happened when I was waiting for her at a bar's pavement table.

A voice behind me asked, "Are you English?"

I replied, "Yes."

The response was, "Well if I bought you a drink, would you tell me about the village?"

Per was a tall, distinguished looking Norwegian, about my age, and we were having an interesting chat when Bea arrived. Gentlemanly Per rushed into the bar to buy her a drink and as they came out, despite it being the end of December, Bea's bulky, warm sweater had been discarded; her white T-shirt was better fitting!

An example of her great sense of humour was, "I'm German down to my neck!"

Later Per was in the Plaza to accept my lift back to Las Américas. In all my wanderings, rarely have I met such an interesting person. We did meet again when I visited Norway and we exchanged Christmas calendars until 2005 when his failed to arrive. I realised that something must have happened when mine was returned with 'Address Unknown' on the envelope.

My first New Year's Eve in Adeje was a surprise because at 2300hrs all was remarkably quiet. Curious, I wandered up the Calle Grande to the Plaza España where a band was playing; couples danced but it wasn't crowded.

It was just before midnight when a family standing next to me asked, "Have you any grapes?"

Puzzled, I answered, "No."

Laughing they said, "Here are twelve grapes. You must eat one with each strike of the clock."

No problem I thought, until I tried. By the twelfth stroke my cheeks were bulging.

Some old men asked me to dance, the people beside me were friendly and I felt as though I was among a larger than average family. Soon a stream of cars began to pour into the village, parking became ever more inventive and some car roofs were covered with table cloths, glasses and bottles of wine; all around, girls in glamorous evening dresses seemed oblivious to the cold. The last band to play stopped at 0900hrs. Standing around were some young men in smart black suits and Father

Christmas hats; empty bottles were on every horizontal ledge and some lonely cars were parked in grotesque positions.

However, the Christmas celebrations did not end on 1st January. On the evening of 5th January it was a joy to watch the faces of excited children as the Three Kings riding on camels threw sweets into the crowd. That evening everyone was rushing around buying elaborately wrapped last minute presents and the Fraga's shop was serving customers well after midnight.

Adeje's Associación San Juan was well hidden but its splendid work was increasingly appreciated. Formed in 1994, it followed the Rudolf Steiner approach that began in 1924. The President, Ana Borges Medina, and Fidel Ortega, the forward-looking Education Director, told me that 20 adults (now increased to 31) with special needs come for work experience, to improve their garden and to look after sheep, goats and hens. Gradually, a restless spirit learns that there is a time for play but also moments to respect a quiet time for thinking. Finances come, often retrospectively after new developments have started, from the Town Halls of Adeje, Guía de Isora and Santiago del Teide, the Canarian and Spanish Governments and not least from money-raising events and donations. The first residential home for five people opened in 2005. By 2008 the centre was being extended and there were plans

The members and friends of Association San Juan
With police escort they begin their walk down from Adeje to the San Sebastián celebrations at the church near La Caleta.

for 800 children, in groups of 70 each day, to visit, integrate and participate in the centre's activities in May.

The hard-working permanent members of staff were assisted by voluntary helpers, young people of both sexes aged from nineteen to twenty two who came from many different countries. Some wanted to get experience before starting professional training in pedagogy while, for a few young men, it was a preferred alternative to a year in the military. For three months they struggled to learn Spanish but the centre's ambience during the Christmas activities helped them to settle in and by Easter many were disturbed at the thought of leaving. Anglican Chaplain Father Keith said that he'd never entered a building with such an atmosphere of love.

No sooner were the Christmas celebrations over than, on 20th January, Adeje celebrated San Sebastián. Roberto, one of the Association's permanent staff, was busy organising the decorations of the goats, sheep and a donkey. Coincidentally, 1996 was both the year that I'd moved into Adeje and, in Adeje's first *La Pasión*, Roberto played Jesus. With local police controlling the traffic, at 1030hrs we set off walking downhill from Adeje to the church near La Caleta at the coast. After the service, at about 1330hrs, the procession left the church and moved slowly down to the sea; here animals and locals received a blessing and dipped their feet into the water.

Police on land and a safety boat offshore ensured that neither enthusiastic visitor photographers nor congregation got washed away, as nearly happened to a horseman one year. The only excitement occurred after the procession had returned to the church. Up the tiled walkway went seventy and a half horses and riders; the half was a miniature pony ridden by a youngster. Most animals were moving in an impressive collected trot but a few were ridden, perhaps as their riders drove, at full speed. The horses' feet scrabbled for purchase on the slippery tiles of the walkway's uphill slope making sparks fly - rear ends were skidding towards spectators!

Adeje's second saint's day, Santa Úrsula, in the second week in October, had ten days of celebrations that required more stamina than I could muster. Throughout six nights, music pulsed and throbbed far and wide until the climax of the 'week', the final Sunday's Romería. The procession started after midday and throughout the two hours that it took to reach the top of the village we played (I'd joined the retired music group) and sang. I competed with my companions for the occasional inch of shade. Food and wine, courtesy of the Town Hall, was distributed from the beautifully decorated carts and that evening everyone settled down to serious talking, drinking and dancing. The music was switched off at midnight. Adeje was a very quiet village!

On the Day of the Trabajadores (the women workers) on the 8th March, an Adeje Consejal (councillor) organised an evening of entertainment for ladies while their menfolk stayed at home looking after the family. At 2000hrs the Cultural Centre's entrance hall was buzzing as guests of the Town Hall wearing glamorous outfits were greeted with a rose and a glass of wine. Soon everyone moved into the lecture theatre and after the usual very flowery language, the precursor of all occasions here, often of a sleep-producing length, the show began. The torrent of words pouring from the mouth of the 'humourista' was way beyond my understanding and, suspecting that this might happen, I'd sat near an exit at the back of the hall. I made my escape unnoticed and it was only next morning that I heard what I had missed. The village was humming with the news that a male striptease artist was the final act of the evening; the following year there were three.

But of all the special days the one that I enjoyed most was the Day of the Retired on 26th July. The Plaza España was full of tables and here I sat with friends and they introduced me to everyone who came to greet them. The wine flowed freely, the food was good, plentiful, all being provided by the Town Hall and served by the hard working, charming staff in the Casa de Mayores (retired centre). The music and the comradeship were unforgettable.

My first encounter with the Santa Cruz Big Carnival was when, on the late night bus returning to my apartment in Los Cristianos with driver Martín, passengers entered wearing weird costumes and butterfly wings brushed my face. Whistle-blowing youngsters in fancy dress were en route to a night of fun.

Martín asked, "Why don't you go to the Carnival?"

"No way, I'm not going there alone," was my immediate response.

To which Martín retorted, "If you went you'd not be on your own for long!"

I never had sufficient courage to go to the Carnival fifty miles away so I was delighted when bar owner Stephan invited me to join him and his family in Santa Cruz for the Carnival's big parade on Tuesday. It started at about 1600hrs but there were long gaps between each elaborately decorated cart and, much as I enjoyed the experience, there was too much standing around. I didn't go again. I could see it on Canarian television in the comfort of my apartment.

It was when wandering around Adeje one evening that the sound of music attracted me. Rarely could I stand still for long, but I was rooted to a spot, for an hour, on the pavement outside Adeje's Cultural Centre watching a superb teacher at work. In José Luis Estevez, Guicho's, class there were smiles, laughter and obvious enjoyment. I ached to be there among them. Perhaps I could learn to play the guitar? I mentioned this to Fernando Berravente; we'd met when I was commuting to Santa Cruz, and he said that he knew where there was a damaged guitar. Generously he repaired it, gave it to me and my dream came true.

When young I'd wanted to learn to play the piano; we couldn't afford one and Granny wouldn't lend us hers. But to enrol in Guicho's class wasn't easy either. I missed a year because I was told that Guicho was teaching in a village several kilometres away. When I got there, the man in charge, not Guicho, ignored me until eventually I approached him with the guitar in my hand, asked for advice and was shown two chords. I didn't return but the following year I joined Guicho's class in Adeje. Here I was advised to buy a book with the chords, doh, ray, mi, laid out clearly on a page and with this and a little tape cassette on which I recorded the songs I practised in my apartment.

At first I'd just move my fingers from one chord to another until I could do this without looking. Then, with the recording, I practised the tune over and over again until my playing matched the music and I could keep up with the class, just. As my folder swelled to fifty lovely Canarian songs I found it impossible to play by ear: I needed the song sheets. I never overcame this weakness or my dread of Malaqueñas, a song that sits uncomfortably in European ears but whose umpteen verses were very popular with Canarians. Even Olivia Stone called it 'the everlasting 'Malagueña'!

It was in Guicho's class that I met many wonderful local people. Teresa Santana Luis noticed that because some of the class persisted in

Early bread delivery

banging loudly on drums, timples and guitars while Guicho was speaking, I was struggling to hear, never mind to understand.

Teresa not only helped me in lessons but also invited me to join her family when they celebrated her daughter Adriana's first communion in May. There were 70 youngsters and, so that all the families and their relatives could fit into the church, two services were held. For three years classes had been held both in and after school to prepare the young people for their big day. For parents it was the culmination of a lot of work and expense. Teresa had paid about 300 Euros (£207) for their oldest daughter Daniela's confirmation dress two years earlier.

After the service about 50 relatives and friends gathered under the tree in their garden for a splendid meal that was well lubricated with good wine from Icod, Teresa's hometown. Afterwards, Adriana circulated, carrying an attractive bag from which she gave every guest mementos of her big day: a Foto Teide photograph of herself, a card and a beautifully crocheted miniature sombrero made by Teresa, a very talented needleworker. My regret was that Teresa couldn't use her talent to earn money because cleaning apartments had caused severe arthritis in her wrists. Family gatherings were always very special and the following year I was honoured to be invited to the first communion of Cristina and José's son, Borja, and their family celebration afterwards.

I'd discovered Guicho's group but it was Cathy Ibbett, she'd lived in Adeje for some years, who told me that there was a retired locals' music group. I found them; their teacher, Mari Carmen, welcomed me and immediately a lady – later she told me that her name was Paca - impressed me with her kindness. Not only did she invite someone she'd never met before to share her song sheet but also afterwards she had music photocopied for me. No one spoke English and from then on, with their patience and help, my Spanish improved; I'd found many friends in these twice weekly classes held in the Casa de Mayores. I never would have believed that I could have so much fun learning 'catchy' Canarian folk songs including the popular 'Maria Cristina'. Not knowing the meaning of all the words didn't matter.

I was lucky that Paca had been to the UK to visit her son Damien, so, unlike most people in the class, she appreciated how our climate and life styles differed to theirs.

Regularly, at about 1300hrs, I'd pop round to Paca's neighbour's house, calling out "La cafetería esta abierta?"("Is the café open?")

Here Mari Lola would serve delicious coffee to Paca, Rosario, myself and sometimes through the window to Paca's husband, Juan, standing outside in the street.

Seeing foreigners prancing around in local costumes looked to my eyes incongruous but Mari Carmen insisted that to go with our group to local fiestas I must have one. Miguelina Barrules, we'd met at the church service near the Parador del Teide, altered one of my cotton blouses and Lala, Candelaria Rodríquez, a neighbour, transformed into a skirt the yards of white cotton lawn that I'd bought in the UK and had dyed a cheerful cherry red. The traditional long skirt had two 'open' panels from waist to hip; from here the side seams were joined down to the hem. The back panel was tied in front then the other was tied behind my back. This allowed the skirt to fit all stages of pregnancy! The pañuelo, headscarf, was made from the white cotton remnant and Mari Carmen found me a hat.

There followed some of my most memorable days and evenings in the company of these kind and generous people. We sang at fiestas in Escalona, Alcalá and other villages, mostly in the hot summer evenings; it was a unique privilege to be the only foreigner in the group. When we flew to La Palma for two nights, Mari Carmen ensured that by standing at the Los Rodeos airport boarding gate we were first onto the plane! The only minus on these excursions was that my stomach needed sustenance long before Canarian lunch at 1500hrs and evening meal at 2100hrs!

Our day-trip to Gran Canaria on a fast ferry from Santa Cruz included a coach trip up the mountain, time to admire the huge wooden doors in the old town and, after an excellent meal, to sing with a local group. I never ceased to be fascinated watching our oldest member, Don Pedro, playing the lout, an instrument that he'd learned to play by ear when he was young. Although well into his eighties and walking with a pronounced arthritic limp, his suggestive wolf whistle had followed me when first I came to Adeje. Since his death I miss chats - when we were sitting in the busy Plaza - with this splendid character!

Traditional music, dances and costumes thrive now thanks to intensive research done by the Folklore Group in Santa Cruz. About 30 years ago they began to investigate the records kept by Alfred Diston (1793-1861). He was born in Lowestoft, came to live in Tenerife and married a distinguished lady, Doña Soledad Orea de Luna-Vargas. From about 60 folios, papers, containing information about fiestas and costumes of the island, a book was produced in 1859.

At first the costumes were controlled by the Guilds but, by the 18th century, workers copied the styles of the wealthy, and they were also influenced by the diverse cultures brought to the islands by so many travellers. In Gran Canaria and in Tenerife, costumes changed with the fashion of the day, whilst in El Hierro, Lanzarote and La Palma, due to their geographical remoteness, their costumes retained their own unique style and individuality. The original materials used in Tenerife were satin, wool and linen; however, outside influences enriched them with lace and embroidery and this has become accepted as a natural development in the costume craft and an inherent part of the folklore tradition.

When Paca told me about the delightful, very popular, folklore programme '*Tenderete*' on Channel 2 for an hour on Sunday nights, I became an addicted viewer. Broadcast from a different village every week we were thrilled when it was recorded in Adeje's Plaza España. Wearing our costumes we had good seats. The well-briefed presenter, Antonio, chatted with local people in between the intervals of music and dancing. It made Sunday night viewing a delight especially if Mari Carmen or Benito Cabrera, the internationally famous timple player, was performing. This instrument has become a solo instrument in its own right and with an orchestra. It was mesmerising to watch this man's fingers dancing over the five strings of his miniature guitar.

When the programme '*La Azotea*' was broadcast from the rooftop of a house in Taucho, this time it was our group who played and sang, and when Trio Chabor (three musicians) played, Paca and I danced together with the magnificent backdrop of La Gomera. Thanks to Cristina videoing the programmes, I have a permanent record of this happy day. Like everyone I spoke to I was heartbroken when, at Easter 2007, mainland Spain took control of, and changed, the television broadcasts in the Canary Islands. At the end of his last programme, an emotional Antonio ran from the cameras. Tenderete continued with a new presenter on Thursdays.

Equal fun, but different, was the annual get-together of retired folk groups from all around the island. About 2,000 of us gathered in the newly built large Centro Ferial de Santa Cruz; it was designed by Santiago Calatrava as was the Auditorium. Here the queues for toilets were almost as long as the twelve lines of tables that extended from front to back of the huge ground floor space! Immediately on arrival huge food hampers were unpacked, and from then on some serious eating and drinking was interrupted only when it was our turn to go onstage. Mari Carmen's wise choice of tunes ensured that our performance was well received - another wonderful day out!

Thanks again to Mari Carmen, our pre-Christmas coach journey was to the north to admire the innumerable hours of work that must have gone into creating the varied Nativity scenes (Belenes). They were well hidden in most towns and many villages. Near Santa Cruz a Belén had many figures, animals in farmyards, fields and a running stream, the total covering an impressively large area of open ground. Later, during our concert in the Santa Rita home for the elderly, I heard for the first time two old men demonstrating the La Gomera 'silbo', whistling, a method of passing messages over long distances. Now silbo has been introduced into the school curriculum in La Gomera and silbo competitions have been started.

Mari Carmen taught in the Luther King College and she introduced me to Sandra Brito, their skilled English-language teacher, whose one hundred students had been split into small groups to study the UK and to give talks; I was their honoured guest. To stand on a stage and talk in a foreign language to teachers, classmates and some parents took courage and impressively even the less fluent students took part. Tania Alegre and Sofía Garrido's brilliant idea was to video interviews with British visitors of differing ages in Las Américas. An old retired couple 'loved to explore the island', some young, tattooed and single people 'loved the nightlife' and some over-weight and under-dressed middle-aged couples were here 'to relax'!

Music was not the only activity in the Casa de Mayores; others included yoga, gymnastics and my equal favourite with Mari Carmen's class was senderismos (walks). As we progressed slowly along the Barranco del Infierno, my friemds were amused when I told them about my recent visit. Two local policemen were rushing to a reported 'dog incident'. No person had been badly bitten but by the waterfall there were four very happy male dogs and one unhappy female. Although it was now a protected area, the protests of our guide did not deter the great character, Mimi, from doing what he'd always done in the countryside, cutting a branch to make it into a walking stick. At the waterfall pool Mimi's invitation to share his 'gasolina', wine, could not be refused, to the amusement of Antonio and Pablo. They worked in the Casa de Mayores and, on our outings, with big smiles they'd order us to return to our coaches at six minutes to the hour, not a minute before or after. It worked!

Our walks were never long because always one or two in the group had difficulty even with pavement walking. But it was relaxed, enjoyable and on every trip I learned something. Stalwart friend, Carmen, had helped me to sing the dreaded Malaqueñas and on an excursion her husband, Tomas Gonzalez Mesa, showed us where salt had been collected beside the Playa San Juan promenade. At a tiny bay, deserted now but for scuba divers, he explained how the remnants of aerial ways had transferred boxes of tomatoes from the land onto boats.

The Casa de Mayores was open weekdays, at times during weekends and was under the control of the Town Hall which provided the dynamic young staff; they stayed here for about two years before moving to do other work for the rapidly expanding numbers of Adeje residents.

Chapter 20
Changes

It was a Saturday evening in May when a long procession of banner-waving cars circled the village with full hand-on-horn attention-seeking accompaniment. It was the first time that I'd seen the four-yearly election of the Mayor. Next morning the street, usually an oasis of tranquillity on a Sunday, was vibrant. Voting was taken seriously and by 2100hrs my plaza was filling with families gathering to hear the results. Horns were blown, drums beaten and the general opinion was that the Mayor, José Miguel Rodríguez Fraga, whose apartment was a few metres from mine, would be re-elected. He was.

Soon after midnight he emerged from his front door into the Calle Grande to celebrate with the crowd. From then on the speed of his progress through my plaza was dictated by the number of greetings he received; from hugs (men) and kisses on the cheek (ladies) his popularity was in no doubt. I wondered how he'd end his walkabout when he entered a side street. A parked car was partly blocking the pavement and cleverly it had left him just enough room to slip into his garage and disappear. But the crowds chanted his name and wouldn't go away. After a suitable delay he emerged onto his balcony and only after Royal-style hand waves to the crowds below would they disperse. He received 78% of the votes.

Four years later, in the days leading up to voting, the Mayor kept me (gathering information for the *Tenerife News*) and the press really busy. At 2200hrs on 20th May in Tijojo, he opened an attractive little museum that recorded the history of the now restored granary. The street party celebrations in meltdown temperatures included an excellent open-air film show, food, wine and music provided by Guicho and the Folklore Group of Adeje. Opening a little library in Calle Grande was a quiet affair and with time running out a new cultural centre in a 'barrio', another part of Adeje, was opened – the work was completed later! At the entrance to Adeje the paving stones' grouting was barely dry when they unveiled the statue of the great Guanche, Gran Tinerfe, who had ruled over Adeje centuries before. Again the mayor was re-elected. Because many locals appreciated the improvements that he'd achieved for Adeje, a change of mayor seemed likely *only* if José Miguel Rodríguez Fraga retired voluntarily.

Of all the village activities I found Easter week the most moving. Religious services were held daily in one barrio or another and an air of quiet expectancy pervaded the village as Laura Marrero, the Directora, held practices for *La Pasión*, the re-enactment of the crucifixion that was broadcast live on television. It was a great and unexpected honour when Laura invited me to participate as one of the crowd.

To ensure punctuality for the evening rehearsals - not all locals' strongest point - this charming lady said, "We meet tomorrow at 9 o'clock, what time do we meet?"

"9 o'clock" was the reply.

"I can't hear you, what time was it?"

"9 o'clock."

And so on.

Throughout the week of preparations, the telephone, lottery kiosks and cameras had been covered and both the camera crew and the support staff – including the man who cleared up horse droppings – would be dressed in robes of the period. In the final practice on Maundy Thursday evening, without crowds or camera flashes, the faces of the watching villagers showed genuine grief as they relived the story. Since the first *La Pasión*, the year that I'd moved into Adeje, the programme had grown until today seventy helpers worked behind the scene and there were over two hundred and fifty actors. On the day, nine manned cameras and numerous photographers were involved.

At noon on Good Friday, words and music introduced the procession led by Roman soldiers on horseback. When all were in place

Jesus, played by a local man from Armeñime, José Lopez Delgado – a relative of Roberto who worked in the Associación San Juan – emerged from a side street on a donkey to ride side saddle up to the Last Supper. This year I joined tour guide Rolf Fuchs and his wife, Dayli, on the balcony of their apartment that was conveniently near the top of the Calle Grande. While waiting for the procession to return downhill to my plaza, I was watching the crowd while Rolf popped into his lounge.

Then he called to me, "Barbara, you're on television and you're scratching!"

As Jesus made his way slowly back down the Calle Grande to my plaza, the change of mood, his cries, questions and the standard of singing were sincere, moving and very well done. From dragging the cross into the Plaza to his being raised upon it and taken down, the 90 minutes were sincere and very affecting. My congratulations go to Laura, the Directora for the last few years, Jose, his fellow actors, to all involved and not least to the Mayor, José Miguel Rodríquez Fraga, and the Town Hall for their initiative.

In the early 1990s there were no big supermarkets in the south, so locals with transport drove north to Continente or Al Campo for a 'big shop'; many people frequented the two family grocers in the Calle Grande. After pay day at the end of the month, the supermarkets were swarming with shoppers - as were the banks on the days when the retired and those on the dole collected their money.

I suppose that it was inevitable that, following the phenomenal rate of building in the south, the busy family grocers disappeared from the Calle Grande. An internet café, the excellent Barbara's bookshop – no relative – and a driving school office arrived. It was good to see that it was not long before some tiny shops opened in the side streets and soon a health centre catered for the increasing number of residents. There were dramatic changes in the north too. In 1901 trams started running between Santa Cruz and La Leguna; they were removed about fifty years later and now they have returned, to the discomfort of those living nearby.

It was in 2003 that I lost three aspects of my life here that I valued highly. To go to the Cañadas for good company and information even when I owned a car, I drove only as far as the first 342 bus stop in Las Américas - to ensure 'my' front seat! Arcadio told me all the local news and often I went for a walk with some of his passengers. Together with the stunning scenery, it was not only a wonderful day out but also it cost a paltry 6-7 Euros using a Bono ticket. Now, due to spondylosis in his neck, Arcadio failed his medical; he ceased driving and became an inspector. I go occasionally to the Cañadas with Antonio, who took over from Arcadio, or Carlos who is an enthusiastic mountaineer. But Arcadio's bus has been replaced by one with the horror of airborne travel, anti-social reclining seats; a much needed improvement is being introduced, new buses have the driver and the money safely behind a security door.

Sadly, in 2003 Mari Carmen suffered a severe throat problem and she could not train our retired group in the Casa de Mayores. I was devastated because with her went the fun of both her classes and the enjoyable excursions. From then on the session was very structured. Every lady (there were never fewer than fifteen) sang her verses of 'Malagueñas' and by the end the guitar player's fingers were aching with the constant repetition of chords. I didn't go again.

As if the loss of Mari Carmen wasn't enough, that year Guicho also stopped teaching our night school classes in the Cultural Centre, although he continued to train the Folklore Group of Adeje. Guicho's classes had overflowed, but now rarely did we play more than two tunes in the hour. Inevitably class attendance plummeted and I was left with a folder of fifty wonderful tunes. Fortunately, a superb musician, Neil Browning from Caernarfon, accepted my request for help. With the aid of the Spanish words he put the tunes I'd recorded in Guicho's class onto a CD. Now, as I accompany the Canarian tunes on my guitar at home in Bangor, a lump comes in my throat.

In the early 1990s I'd seen no walkers in the Cañadas or on the paths at lower altitude. Gradually I began to meet leaders, usually Germans, who were followed by a line of well equipped enthusiasts. Today a glance at the internet shows a profusion of advertisements for guided walks in Tenerife. Harder to find were the qualifications of the 'guides', whether they were insured or if their clients were taken to walks in their licensed vehicle or by bus.

At first, cyclists putting their bicycles in the luggage compartment of Arcadio's bus in Los Cristianos was a rare occurrence. Now this happens quite often because Tenerife has been 'discovered' as a popular base both for athletes to train and for 'activity' holidays. Vilaflor, at 5000ft (1524m), has a new hotel, Villalba, and among its many excellent facilities there is a climbing wall. Regularly, in winter, a rather portly man wearing shorts and a safari hat sat ramrod upright, straight-backed on a bicycle as he led a group of cyclists down the El Teide road to Vilaflor; a van and trailer for the bikes followed. Throughout the descent his knees were positioned outwards; a picture of a frog immediately sprang into my mind and this is one of the two photographs that I regret having missed. (The other was the police speed-monitoring Arrive Alive van when it was parked outside Bangor's crematorium.)

It was inevitable that with the new roads have come changes. The homogenising of Tenerife to resemble any other sun-rich resort had been relentless and for years the travel writers in the UK newspapers were consistent in their comments. At best they advised visitors wanting peace and quiet to avoid the British bars and drunks, to go to La Gomera. Then, in the spring of 2008, a *Sunday Times* two-page article told readers to avoid the overcrowded coastline and buy building land in Tenerife's lovely countryside, at El Chorro. The vendor was a relative of my friends, Blanca and Hucho, with whom I'd shared those wonderful Sundays. Coincidentally in the same month a euphoric presenter on UK television raved about Tenerife's climate, saying that it had 'all year round sunshine'.

This horrified me because few – if any – places in the world have a perfect, clear blue sky every day. Rather than raising visitors' expectations – Tenerife is still being sold, by some travel agents, as having 'all the year round perfect climate' – it would be better to be honest. Even in May some places in the Canary Islands can have temperatures reaching 38°C; in summer it gets hotter, and occasionally fires have seriously damaged some beautiful areas of the countryside. They *do* have rain in winter and old ladies in black dresses told me that the barrancos used to run with water at that time of year. The weather can be cloudy and occasionally a vicious wind can, and does, cause damage. Last winter, winds felled about half the pylons on El Hierro, leaving locals without electricity while La Calima comes from nearby Africa bringing dust of varying severity, heat and sometimes vicious winds. This seems to be happening more often, in any month and for longer. Despite all this, without doubt, the weather in Tenerife in winter is warmer than at home, in Northern Europe, and arthritis sufferers often find relief in this climate.

However (water supplies permitting) I hope that in this Year of the Potato their delicious Canarian potatoes (papas arrugadas), will thrive. John Reader's fascinating book, *The Propitious Esculent,* tells us that this crop has four times more calories than grain sown on the same sized plot of land and that the potato came from South America to the Canary Islands in the 1560s. From here records show that in 1572 potatoes arrived in Antwerp and then they spread across Europe - a challenge to the Walter Raleigh, Francis Drake story!

Since I rented an apartment in Adeje village not only have many Canarians introduced me to their way of life, but also they have become stalwart friends. Their spontaneous welcomes are unfailing and always much appreciated, while the kindness of the majority of the TITSA drivers remains impressive. I live in hope that *soon* TITSA bosses will improve visitors' experiences in Tenerife by ensuring the *prompt* replacement of *all* out-of-date information with an *accurate* timetable at *every* bus stop in the south!

Now that my three score years and ten has arrived, I look back and realise how lucky my generation has been; what was impossible yesterday is today's commonplace. When I started mountaineering, unclimbed crags were waiting to be explored, exciting first ascents of new routes were there to be plucked and I knew many females who climbed hard routes. Without meeting Ron I doubt if I would have been one of them. (Also, without Ron and Ginny's help with my computer problems over the years, I might not have written this book.) Our mountaineering equipment was very basic compared to today but luckily for us the technical developments have improved as we've got older. Modern protection has reduced rock climbers' injuries from falls while hill walkers' risk of hypothermia in severe weather is less thanks to superb quality, light weight waterproofs and good footwear; today a drink can be carried within a jacket lining.

Sadly however, despite all these improvements, the availability of training courses, excellent weather forecasts and navigation aids such as the GPS (some now accept Ordnance Survey maps, at a cost), nearly

Three years' work
Unable to spot all the errors on the computer screen, I printed every page,

75% of Ogwen Valley Mountain Rescue Organisation's callouts recently were for uninjured walkers. While mobile phones enable rapid response for the seriously injured, they also provide an easy option for the incompetent, the incapable and the downright lazy. In the UK hills there have been relatively few tragedies over which those with no knowledge get worked up; those with experience learn and consider. All too often a serious situation can become a crisis when the *inconvenient* decision, to turn back, is made too late and the result is the unnecessary loss of life among both mountaineers and pilots.

Today the hills have become alive with the sound of bikes, two-wheeled and quad! On Snowdon there is a voluntary ban on mountain bikers, daytime 1000-1700hrs from the end of May to September and a group of *mono* bikers has been seen ascending the mountain. Activity centres now number around two hundred, Snowdon's Miners and Pyg tracks cater for 160,000 people per annum, and infra-red counters on paths record those passing – but not sheep! The information is useful for the allocation of much needed finances for path maintenance and in suitable places for disabled access. Yearly the numbers of hill walkers have increased while today many rock climbers are introduced to the sport through the countrywide *indoor* facilities. The British Mountaineering Council runs some excellent events. Their Youth Climbing Series is for the fun and enjoyment of youngsters, while the British Bouldering Competitions (double and triple density foam mats can be bought to soften landings) and the British Lead Climbing Championships are very popular.

The outstanding climber, Reinholt Messner, is an example of the compulsion each generation has to improve upon the successes of their predecessors. In 1978, with Peter Habeler, he made the first ascent of Everest without oxygen; in 1980 he returned here solo and without oxygen and in 1987, aged 42, he became the first man to climb all the fourteen 8,000m peaks in the Himalayas. Alan Hinks was the first British climber to achieve this goal. The Eiger was first climbed in 1858 and since then its history is remembered mainly for the epic ascents and fatalities on its north face. In April 2008 I read that it had been speed-climbed by Swiss mountaineer, Uri Steck, in 2 hours 47 minutes 33 seconds; he'd broken his own record, made in 2007, of just less than four hours.

Meanwhile, today, to be the first to 'do' something requires ever more inventive ideas. Not satisfied with entering the *Guinness Book of Records* for travelling the length of Great Britain on his longboard, the Land Rover of skateboards, Dave Comthwaite skated the 4,500 miles from Perth to Brisbane.

My generation has lived through enormous changes in dissemination of knowledge, from the wireless to television and the internet to instant communication via mobile phones. Medical procedures also have improved dramatically. My father had refused the heart operation that he needed when he was told that the success rate was at best 50%. Today's clever surgery would have given him many more years of active life. If I could have three wishes they would be *not* to have been left on steroid pills for fifteen years, that my mother could have died working in her garden as she'd wished and that my father had known about my Private Pilot's Licence.

Looking back, I'm grateful to Major Stuart Thornborough, the Senior Education Officer, who courageously appointed me, probably the first civilian female to train infantry soldiers. During those eleven challenging years I *had* to find ways to survive solo travel. Aching for company, I did speak to strangers on a train, take risks, meet some interesting people and accumulate some unwise, but many outstanding, experiences. It was a great relief to escape from the Kentish breezes full of oil seed rape pollen and it was no surprise that the severity of my eczema lessened only after I'd left behind the stresses of work and commuting. But, without my years with the military, I doubt if I'd have had the magical holiday in the Falkland Islands. Here, thanks to meeting Chris Francis in Stanley, I learned to fly a plane and had the outstanding experience of flying a Cessna solo around Florida.

My idea, for an exhibition about the history of British mountaineering that might lead to a national data base, was coming to fruition, thanks to the hard work of famous climber, George Band, and many others. Coincidentally, protest about the government's handling of the foot and mouth was at its height so for security reasons the opening at Rheged, near Penrith, by Tony Blair was kept a secret until the very last minute. The day chosen was 26th July 2001.

By then the school holidays had started. The years of driving between Folkestone and Bangor in all weathers and in school holiday traffic had left me with a severe aversion to travelling anywhere, certainly not by plane to Tenerife in August. Luckily that summer the UK's dreaded pollen season wasn't severe and I realised that my eczema was calmer away from the summer heat of Tenerife and from then on I went there only after my friends said that 'winter has arrived'. Nowadays this is in December when, hopefully, the daytime temperature is below 25°C. With the wisdom of hindsight, much as I've enjoyed mountaineering and discovering the real Tenerife, with both eczema and an allergy to my own sweat, I did pay for my pleasures with my health.

When young I hated being different from the other children but it had to be endured. My hope is that those of us with eczema, allergies and sensitive skin will receive greater understanding of our problem in the future. It is possible to avoid colourings, flavourings, excessive sugar and the other unnecessary extras that the food industry inflicts upon us, by eating recognisable meat and fresh fruit and vegetables. For a chocoholic it is a relief that most people now know not to say, "Eat it, there are *only a few* nuts/sesame seeds in the chocolate."

Unfortunately today the majority of '100% cotton' clothing manufacturers have become addicted to *only a few* 'improvements'. The blouses have non-iron chemicals, the cotton trousers have 3% elastane (or 1% spandex) and the cotton socks have anti-fungal chemicals so that they won't smell; I thought we had washing machines to remove that problem! The only true 100% cotton, or linen, clothes that are not 'improved' are 'casual' trousers (two long tubes held together with a square at the top), jeans and blouses in stripes and checks.

I hope that soon everyone with very sensitive skin will have not only a *choice* of 100% *un*improved cotton clothes, in a variety of colours and styles, to choose from but also that, when asked for a dog-free hotel room, a receptionist will never reply, "Only small dogs stay here."